D1243954

A Christian's guide to leadership
— for the whole church

A Christian's guide
to leadership
— for the whole church

Derek Prime

EVANGELICAL PRESS

EVANGELICAL PRESS
Faverdale North, Darlington, DL3 0PH, England

e-mail: sales@evangelicalpress.org

Evangelical Press USA
P. O. Box 825, Webster, New York 14580, USA

e-mail: usa.sales@evangelicalpress.org

web: www.evangelicalpress.org

First published 2005

British Library Cataloguing in Publication Data available

ISBN 0 85234 602 6

Printed and bound in Great Britain by Creative Print and Design, Ebbw Vale, South Wales.

Contents

Introduction

The first version of this book was written more than forty years ago when I was at the beginning of pastoral responsibility. These many years later I am even more aware of the need for encouraging and training people for leadership. One of the most exciting and enriching experiences has been to have a succession of younger men as assistants and to be allowed to contribute to the preparation for their life's work. The joy of seeing their contributions to the church of our Lord Jesus Christ throughout the world is immense. After thirty years as a pastor, the last seventeen years have been spent serving churches in the UK and sometimes overseas. Inevitably people have shared problems and challenges, of which a huge percentage have proved to be issues of leadership.

There are many kinds of leadership, although they all have much in common. Christian leadership, however, has two important distinctives that make it not only different but sometimes poles apart from all other forms. The Christian leader is always and completely subject to the Lord Jesus Christ who is the ultimate Leader or Head of the church. His leadership is neither vague nor theoretical but extremely practical. He exercises this leadership primarily through his

Word, the Scriptures. Those who lead in the church must accept the authority of that Word and be thorough and wholehearted in their obedience to it. Their vision and objectives — and the way in which they aim to achieve them — must be shaped and determined by his Word.

The particular concern of this book is leadership within the local church. It has in view pastors and those who fulfil the tasks of elders and deacons, even though these names and titles may not be used. It has also in its sights the leaders of young people's work and those directing other important areas of church life. I particularly want to encourage young people to prepare and equip themselves for leadership. Much of what we establish will be relevant to other spheres of Christian leadership, but the immediate area of application of principles will be the community of Christians gathered in a local church.

You may be wondering whether it is rather presumptuous to read a book on leadership if you are not already a leader. This book arises out of a belief that it is not conceited to be interested in the subject. That assurance is based upon three considerations:

- most of us have to share at times in the choice and appointment of leaders;
- we have to work under the leadership of others;
- we ourselves may be called to leadership in the future.

Carefully-appointed leaders are essential to the spiritual well-being of the people of God; and God gives his people the responsibility of giving official recognition to those whom he provides. As workers, although not leaders, we need to know what to expect of those who have a leadership role and how best to assist them. Furthermore, since leadership may be thrust upon us at any moment, an element of preparedness is invaluable if we are to rise to its challenge.

When Field Marshal Montgomery, a famous leader of the British Forces during the Second World War, contemplated writing his book *The Path to Leadership*, he relates how he mentioned the fact to a friend, whose reply was, 'I will give you the same advice often given to a man contemplating matrimony: don't.' Nothing daunted, the field marshal proceeded with his task, well aware of its difficulty. Leadership remains a difficult subject to handle; that fact we freely admit. Opinions vary as to what constitutes leadership. If a group of people is asked to list leadership qualities, matters such as personality, demeanour, intellectual ability, enthusiasm, natural gifts and other qualities will be suggested priorities in a varying order of significance.

The difficulty of our subject probably points to its import-ance. Happily, our task is easier than that of Field Marshal Montgomery, because we are concerned with spiritual leader-ship within the Christian church. As a result, we have a reliable and authoritative guide since all the basic principles of such leadership are found in the Bible, and not a few of the problems of the early church throw light upon our subject. In addition, we may rely upon the Holy Spirit's help as we endeavour to apply biblical principles to our contemporary situation.

Two sets of questions are to be found at the conclusion of each chapter, including this introduction: the first for Bible study groups, and the second for church leaders.

The questions for the *Bible study groups* are based upon both the chapter and the chosen Bible passages.

The questions for *church leaders* could well be used — a chapter at a time — at the beginning of regular meetings of church leaders, with their conclusions forming part of their agenda, where appropriate.

Prayer

Almighty God, we recognize the folly of beginning any endeavour trusting our human ability. By your gracious Holy Spirit, the sovereign dispenser of your gifts, enlighten our minds as we consider the subject of leadership. Enable us to appreciate all that is good and part of your common grace in the examples we see in the world and help us to see what is distinctive about the leadership that has the Lord Jesus Christ as its model. Give us the courage we need to expose ourselves to your Word. We ask this through Jesus Christ our Lord. Amen.

Questions for Bible study groups

Read Exodus 17:8-15; 24:12-18; Numbers 11:28; 27:12-23

1. How is Joshua described in his relationship to Moses? What does that term or title say about training for leadership?
2. How deliberate was the training of Joshua for leadership? How was it achieved?
3. What vital lessons about leadership did Joshua learn from Moses?

Read Acts 16:1-5; 18:1-11; 1 Timothy 4:12-16; 2 Timothy 2:1-7

4. What preparation did Timothy have for leadership?
5. Was youth a disqualification for leadership? What was more important than Timothy's age?
6. What was to be a priority in Timothy's exercise of leadership?

7. How would you define the main characteristics of good leaders?

Questions for church leaders

1. *In what ways are we deliberately encouraging and training people for leadership and how can we do this more?*
2. *How many of our current problems and challenges are issues of leadership?*

1.
The necessity for leadership

We only have to think of what happens when there is no leadership to recognize its necessity. Imagine a class without a teacher; or an army without a general; or a government without a prime or first minister.

I began my adult life as a teacher, working at first in one school for a term and then in another for three years. The life of the first was somewhat chaotic and certainly not attractive. The second was happy, ordered and disciplined in its life and, fortunately for me, it was there that I worked the longer. On reflection, it was the head teacher who made the difference. He established the principle that the school had only one rule: 'Every boy should behave as a gentleman.' That sounds rather quaint and totally unrealistic in today's culture. We may ask, 'How on earth did he get away with it? How did he make it work?' The answer is that he genuinely meant it and exemplified good behaviour in the way he dealt with both staff and boys.

Without leadership, little is done properly; and unnecessary duplication can occur with several people doing the same job, wasting energy and time. It is then not long before friction results from the general chaos that reigns, as it threatened to do early on in the church's history (Acts 6:1).

Leaders are essential if only to avoid such chaos, prevent duplication, get things done and nip any friction in the bud. The task of settling the Israelites into their inheritance in the land of Canaan was a massive undertaking, fraught with potential complications and conflicts. Significantly, God instructed Moses to appoint *one* leader from each tribe to help assign the land to the people (Numbers 34:16-29). Establishing such leadership was part of God's blessing of Israel. His judgement upon his people's sin — and society's rebellion against him in general — may sometimes be the disappearance of genuine leadership (Isaiah 3:1-7). Those with a desire and capacity to bring men and women together in harmony to achieve a common purpose are always necessary. Without them, there is little hope of doing things 'in a fitting and orderly way' (1 Corinthians 14:40).

Leadership is necessary everywhere

Every sphere of Christian service requires the best leadership available and the church cannot be healthy without it. Take, for example, the worldwide missionary enterprise of the church as she endeavours to fulfil the Lord Jesus Christ's final commission. If leaders are not trained within missions, missionaries are then unlikely to encourage nationals in leadership; yet, if the latter development does not take place, the national church will not grow and develop as it ought. Whether we think of the spiritual oversight of the local church, the administrative responsibilities of her corporate life or the many and varied activities that take place within her buildings, the more suited to leadership people are, the more effective will be the work and witness of the church. What is true of the local church also applies to all other situations where Christians work together.

Familiar problems are often those of leadership

An in-depth questionnaire on far-reaching issues affecting the contemporary church reported, 'Major church issues were fundamentally relational, arising either from overbearing, heavy-handed leadership, or non-existent, "fuzzy" leadership, or simply because the church was cursed by the kind of power games that were more readily associated with the workplace.'[1] The friction caused by issues such as these is all too common. Tension between individuals as they work together is inevitable to a degree; but sometimes it happens because leaders have not learnt the basics of harmonious personal relationships.

In order to persist when faced with a difficult task — a priority in all Christian work — people need constant inspiration and encouragement; and if these are lacking, many will flounder. Such a situation usually reveals a deficiency in leadership: the leader has not learned to inspire confidence. Colin Powell, a US Secretary of State, was involved as a soldier in the training of tank crews. He makes the significant observation that 'The battalions that did best were those with the best commanders. A good commander could motivate his men to excel under any conditions ... The new technologies were adopted, and they did make a difference. But we never lost sight of the reality that people, particularly gifted commanders, are what make units succeed ... The way I like to put it, leadership is the art of accomplishing more than the science of management says is possible.'[2] Inefficiency is not an uncommon problem. That is not to suggest that leaders are lazy or deliberately inefficient, but rather that they may try to do too much themselves and fail to delegate. As soon as inefficiency arose in the administration of the corporate life of the early church, delegation took place (Acts 6:1-6). This sets an important example.

Lack of co-ordination is a frequent difficulty; there can be individuals and organizations within the same church fellowship all working as if their work were its sole activity. This implies that those in charge have not applied the principles governing working and co-operating together as a team. Many of us have had the experience of watching an activity getting into an almost hopeless rut and ending up proving more or less useless. More often than not, this predicament arises from a lack of direction and enthusiasm on the part of the leadership.

Fortunately, most of these areas of difficulty may be anticipated and avoided; and it is one of the hopes and purposes of this book to give that help.

The need for leaders is urgent

The church of our Lord Jesus Christ is desperately in need of leaders. Dr Sangster, an outstanding twentieth-century Methodist leader, wrote in the early days of his ministry, 'The Church is painfully in need of leaders. I wait to hear a voice and no voice comes. I love the back seat in Synod and Conferences. I would always rather listen than speak — but there is no clarion voice to listen to.' His main concern here was with the 'top-leadership' of the church rather than our first interest, the local church; but the lack of outstanding leaders in the church as a whole is a symptom of the health of the church in its local context.

A well-known Scottish journalist, Harry Reid, was commissioned to interview many of the leaders and people of the Church of Scotland and look at the state of the church. One of the clear conclusions that emerged from his interviews, such as one he had with a university principal, was that 'the

Kirk needs to pay more serious attention to encouraging and training its leaders, present and future … Leadership is essential if the Church of Scotland is to arrest its decline.'[3]

Too many leave too much to too few

Generalizations are always open to correction but it is not unfair to say that too many often let too few do all the work and take all the responsibility. Someone has written, 'I have a vivid memory of a day when, as children, we were playing together at the side of a London canal. Our rubber ball went in, and bobbed about tantalizingly near the bank. Small David was urged to reach for it. Obediently I crouched perilously on my haunches and stretched for all I was worth — and just touched it. "Go on," hissed my elder sister fervently. "You're there!" And I was, for as she spoke she gave me an encouraging push and the next moment I had my first experience of total immersion.'[4] Not a few 'elder sisters or brothers' allow the minority to carry too heavy a load of responsibility. This is not to criticize them but rather to point out that they are not developing their own potential for leadership and that as a result activities 'plod' rather than progress.

New Testament teaching

The New Testament implies that recognized leadership is fundamental to the church's spiritual development and health. Careful and detailed instructions are given concerning qualifications required of those appointed to the office of elder or overseer (1 Timothy 3:1-13; Titus 1:6-9). The choice of

suitable leaders was considered a number-one priority (Acts
14:23; Titus 1:5). The standards laid down for the particular
functions mentioned should be those aimed at by all who would
exercise any form of leadership within the church of Christ; we
examine those standards in our third chapter.

Circumstances requiring leadership

Everywhere in the New Testament, the need for leadership
finds expression. Progress in the preaching of the gospel and
the evangelization of the world demands it. Matthias was
appointed to take the place of Judas (Acts 1:25-26), while the
church at Jerusalem recognized that Paul was to take the lead
in conveying the gospel to the Gentiles, and Peter to the Jews
(Galatians 2:9). Leadership is necessary for discipline; it needs to
be someone's designated responsibility to deal with difficulties
that arise in the corporate life of God's people. Leadership is
imperative if guidance and decisions are to be given (Acts 15:6;
21:18-25). When a crisis arises, someone has to take action and
that individual needs to be a responsible person.

Cohesion and co-ordination depend upon leadership; if the
leaders of the early church had not co-ordinated the activities
of Paul and Peter (Galatians 2:9), church history would have
been detrimentally different. The Christian faith has to be
defended from many kinds of attack; and leadership, in the
right hands (1 Timothy 3:9; Titus 1:9), is fundamental to the
maintenance of the truth of the gospel. And we must not
forget that leadership is important if God's people are to be
cared for spiritually, because they need shepherding (1 Peter
5:1-4).

The disciples were potential leaders

In the light of all that the New Testament implies as to the necessity of leadership, it is not surprising that our Lord Jesus Christ spent three years training a small group of potential leaders. He carefully gave them the words of his Father; he provided an example of leadership they never forgot; he taught the principles of leadership and sent them out on training exercises, taking them aside afterwards to discuss all that had happened (Mark 6:30-31). They, in turn, saw it as their duty to train others in the years that followed Pentecost. Yet nowhere, perhaps, is the church of Christ more negligent than in its encouragement and production of leaders.

As we think of those first disciples we may consider them to have been unlikely material, but such a reaction is clearly wrong. David Sheppard, once leader of the Mayflower Family Centre, a pioneer of the Church of England's social work in the inner city, and eventually Bishop of Liverpool, worked as a curate at St Mary's Islington in London. He writes, 'I remember, with shame, saying to a friend, "I don't believe leader types live around here. We can't avoid importing leaders."' He then adds, 'That remark needed to be disowned before I moved on to Mayflower.'[5]

A fundamental principle

A fundamental principle given by Paul to Timothy is translated in the New English Bible as follows, 'To aspire to leadership is an honourable ambition' (1 Timothy 3:1). These words were possibly submitted originally to Paul for his comment, and, if so, he accepts them as good and commendable. The context is the appointment of elders and bishops — these two terms seem to have been used of the same office in the early church — and there are good reasons why Paul should make the comment he did. The title *episcopos* (bishop or overseer) is used of our Lord Jesus Christ (1 Peter 2:25), and to lead his people is to continue his ministry — a high privilege.

Eldership is the oldest religious office in the world. Seventy elders were appointed to assist Moses (Numbers 11:16-30) and the title was used later of those who administered the affairs of the synagogues. The highest standards were required of bishops, elders and deacons in the early church; thus to want to fill these offices means aspiring to holiness and godliness. In times of opposition to the church from the state, leadership in the first century could bring suffering and sacrifice, even as it must, in varying degrees, to Christian leaders in countries where the whole religious or cultural ethos is opposed to Christianity.

To aspire to leadership, out of the highest motives, is an honourable ambition. It demonstrates love for our Lord Jesus Christ and concern for the welfare of his people. It is leadership in the most important sphere in the world since all God's purposes are related in some way or other to his eternal purposes for the church, the Bride of his Son. The highest standards are required; this objective therefore will produce godly character. It is better than any worldly ambition; and it yields eternal dividends.

'Here is a trustworthy saying: If anyone sets his heart on being an overseer, he desires a noble task' (1 Timothy 3:1). This statement alone, besides all the reasons we have given to substantiate it, justifies our emphasizing the worth of leadership.

Prayer

Almighty God, the God and Father of our Lord Jesus Christ, help us to have a right understanding of the necessity of good leadership. May we be kept from exaggerating its importance but at the same time helped to see where some of our problems and difficulties arise from its absence. Help us to develop the spiritual gifts you have given us, not with an eye to our satisfaction but yours and the good of your Son's church. May all our ambitions be good and honourable, for our Lord Jesus Christ's sake.

Questions for Bible study groups

Read Numbers 11:16-30; Isaiah 3:1-9; Acts 6:1-7

1. What was the principal task of the seventy elders in relation to Moses and what was their priority need? How do your conclusions relate to your situation?
2. To what sorts of leadership does Isaiah refer? What kind of things are said to happen when leadership is absent? How might this sometimes be God's judgement upon his people?
3. What problems prompted the choosing of the seven in Acts 6? What qualification was identical to the priority need of the seventy elders? What was the most significant consequence of the appointment of the seven to which Luke refers?
4. What problems arise from the absence of leadership?

Questions for church leaders

1. *Are there specific areas in our church life where leadership is noticeably absent? If so, what positive action can we take? In the short term? In the longer term?*
2. *Where is there unnecessary duplication in our church activities or responsibilities?*
3. *Is there friction among our membership? What has leadership to do with it? What is our responsibility?*
4. *Which individuals in leadership need special encouragement? How can we give it? Who should do it at this present time?*

2.
Essential qualities for spiritual leadership

We do not have to be natural leaders — or born leaders — to exercise spiritual leadership. Many who have never considered they had such gifts have found themselves in the position of spiritual responsibility. An outstanding biblical example is Gideon (Judges 6 – 8). He knew and felt himself utterly unprepared and ill-equipped. In one sense that made him both well prepared and equipped, for like many others described in Hebrews 11 he was one 'whose weakness was turned to strength' (v. 34).

Natural powers of leadership

Spiritual leadership inevitably possesses some relationship to natural powers and abilities. The latter are to be viewed as God-given, as part of what is sometimes called common grace. In spite of human rebellion and sin God chooses to endow men and women with special gifts and talents for the good of all.

If before conversion we led others with relative ease, it is reasonable to expect that such ability will be enhanced and lifted to a higher plane as a result of new spiritual life. From the time the first disciples were called to follow Jesus, it is clear that they often took their lead from Peter. It is no surprise, therefore, to find him taking the lead at Pentecost and afterwards, filled as he then was with the Holy Spirit (Acts 2:4; 4:8). Paul was a principal organizer of the opponents of Christianity before his conversion; not unnaturally, we find him later leading people in the opposite direction.

The difference conversion makes

The history of the Christian church provides ample evidence that spiritual new birth makes leaders of people who probably would never otherwise have become such. The Holy Spirit frequently brings to light natural abilities that have been hidden and stimulates their development. Furthermore, for the well-being of the body of Christ, he imparts spiritual gifts, and for some this will be the gift of leadership (Romans 12:8).

As we have mentioned, spiritual abilities are not always unrelated to natural capabilities; rather, they enhance them and enable them to realize their full potential. What is true of the Christian church was equally the case for God's people in the Old Testament period. A book like Judges demonstrates that spiritual leadership came about through the Holy Spirit coming upon individuals (see, for example, Judges 2:18; 3:9-10, 15). The raising up of leaders was recognized to be a mark or sign of God's good hand upon his people (Ezra 8:18).

Basic qualities

There are certain qualities, the product of God's common grace, which will generally be present in Christian as much as in non-Christian leaders. However, as we shall see, for the Christian leader these qualities on their own are not enough. First, though, let us briefly examine five essential qualities applicable to leadership generally.

1. There must be a distinctive character that inspires confidence and loyalty.

In some measure, leaders should stand out from others, not because they deliberately set out to do this, but on account of the contribution they make whenever they are involved. On a committee, for example, we find that people often give particular attention to what some members say whenever they contribute to a discussion. This is not necessarily because of the positions of special responsibility they hold but because they always have something worthwhile to say and can be depended upon to give a positive and constructive lead. When leadership is necessary, no one will be surprised when these individuals are appointed.

2. There must be a capacity for work and decision-making.

To lead others requires a capacity for making choices. While there is great strength, wisdom and benefit in aiming at *corporate* decisions, there are moments when leaders must recognize that only they can rightly decide and act.

Leadership is never to be regarded as a soft option or a means of gaining 'an easy passage'. Although leaders should endeavour to shift as much routine administrative work as possible from their own shoulders to others, innumerable matters will keep coming to them for decision, as will new developments for assessment and initiative. They should not shelve making decisions; rather they should weigh all the factors and act upon their considered judgement with clarity and energy.

Fear of criticism should not hinder leaders making what they know to be right decisions. The tragic events of 9/11 in New York brought to the fore the leadership of its then mayor, Rudolph Giuliani. Immediate decisions had to be made and he recognized he was the one to make them. He wrote, 'Often I make a decision knowing that I'll be criticized but feeling certain I'll be vindicated. A leader has to have the confidence to think that his decisions will be proven correct. While trying to maintain humility, you must accept that the reason you're making these decisions and other people are not is because, for now, you're in charge and they aren't. You do no one any good if, like Hamlet, you cannot carry the weight of your convictions. Yes, you must guard against arrogance; but if you're doing your job and putting your motives and conscience through their paces, accept that maybe you really do know better and can see a little further down the road than others.'[1]

3. *There needs to be an element of energy and enthusiasm.*

Paul's instruction, 'Never be lacking in zeal, but keep your spiritual fervour, serving the Lord' (Romans 12:11), is relevant to all Christians but especially to leaders. They must be people of 'drive', who get things done: not by doing everything themselves, but through the involvement and assistance of others. Boundless energy is necessary. Their enthusiasm should be infectious and sufficient to overcome the inevitable snags that will crop up to hinder the achievement of their aims. Peter Scott, the painter and naturalist, gave considerable leadership in the area of conservation. He was marked by passion and zeal. 'His enthusiasm for everything to do with conservation or the animal world would warm you like a fire,' was Gerald

Durrell's comment. 'Half an hour with Peter and you felt you could succeed in realizing your wildest dreams.'[2]

4. There should be readiness to assume responsibility for the direction of others.

Many shrink from such duty for different reasons — perhaps through a nervous or anxious temperament, or unwillingness to be completely committed to responsibility that will bring ties and duties. Leaders should never shirk legitimate responsibility: as soon as they do, they cease, in some measure, to be leaders.

5. There needs to be an ability to convey to others a vision and to work with them to see it realized.

If leaders give the appearance of leading simply because they enjoy telling other people what to do, they will not get very far. If, however, they work with a clear goal of achievement and can impart something of it to those with whom they work, they will find ready co-operation and lasting progress. People will be excited at being brought on board and they in turn will excite others. Uncommunicative people who lack vision and enterprise do not make good leaders.

Other qualities could be added to this list, depending upon the situation we have in view, but these represent essential virtues shared by all forms of leadership.

Spiritual leadership

Spiritual leadership is not unrelated to these fundamental qualities since each is necessary. But the immediate point we must make is that decisions relating to the choice of spiritual leaders are not finally determined by any one of these factors but by a dynamic — not yet mentioned — that influences each of these qualities for the good.

The distinctive Christian requirement

The early church had the duty of appointing men to be responsible for the relief of the needy. The apostles instructed the Jerusalem church to consider whom they could appoint. The office was of such importance and delicacy — the care of women and children — that individuals of the highest reputation were required. Administration was a vital part of the task and people of spiritual wisdom were necessary. However, even if men with these qualities were available, more was required: they had to be men 'full of the Spirit' (Acts 6:3).

In fact, that a man should be 'full of the Spirit' is the major requirement for Christian leadership, and an essential difference from all other kinds. However, we immediately face something of a difficulty at this point. No one, we hope, would go around saying, 'I am filled with the Holy Spirit', although hopefully every Christian would want that to be true.

What it means to be filled with the Spirit almost eludes definition and none is found in the Bible. It is not something that we should expect to feel but rather a truth we are meant to exhibit. No one is filled with the Spirit without wanting it to be the case and desiring to live a holy life. It is seen in the fruit of the Spirit — the character of the Lord Jesus — appearing and growing in a Christian's life, since the life and character of the Lord Jesus show us what it means to be filled with the Spirit.

This requirement is another way of expressing the truth that Christian leadership can be exercised in a God-pleasing manner only by those who know and show their complete dependence upon God rather than upon themselves or their gifts. God's people, who have to appoint them or confirm their calling, will recognize this to be true of them since the same Holy Spirit will give them this insight to discern the fruit of the Spirit in their characters and conduct.

Dissimilarities

This distinctive spiritual requirement creates dissimilarities from other kinds of leadership. Christian leaders know themselves to be *under God*. In other spheres, leaders may be under no one and may be a law to themselves. Christian leaders are always to see themselves under the authority of their Master. They are not to act to please themselves. Rather than determining a course of action according to their personal point of view, they must want to act under the direction of God the Holy Spirit. Shepherds though they may be, they are always '*under*shepherds'.

Christ-made leaders

Christian leaders are essentially Christ-made. While they possess natural abilities it is the Holy Spirit who enables them to use them to the benefit of the church. He is Christ's gift to them, as too is his infilling. Christ makes and provides leaders for his church (Mark 1:17; Ephesians 4:7-13). Leaders in other spheres may sometimes describe themselves as self-made or duly qualified because of examinations passed, but not so Christian leaders.

The example of Christ

Christian leadership involves deliberately following another leader — the Lord Jesus Christ. The first leaders of the church heard him say, 'Come, follow me, and I will make you fishers of men' (Mark 1:17). Undershepherds are to model themselves on the Chief Shepherd and this demands that they first be examples to his flock and, secondly, their servants for Christ's sake.

The leader an example

Christian leaders are to be an example to those they lead. Paul's words to Timothy are interesting at this point for after telling Timothy to 'command and teach' — both obvious activities of leadership — he says, 'Don't let anyone look down on you because you are young, but set an example for the believers in speech, in life, in love, in faith and in purity' (1 Timothy 4:12). Peter's instruction to elders has the same thought when he tells them not to lord it over those entrusted to them but to be 'examples to the flock' (1 Peter 5:3). Paul stands out as an ideal leader at this point when he writes, 'Whatever you have learned or received or heard from me, or seen in me — put it into practice. And the God of peace will be with you' (Philippians 4:9). Paul was not being proud or presumptuous to write in such a way. He knew, as every Christian should know, that you cannot instruct others unless you yourself do what you tell them to do. If we have the privilege of working under a good leader for a period of time, in later years in some difficult circumstance or crisis we will find ourselves asking, 'What would he have done in this situation?'

Christian leaders should not only be able to speak of a Christian lifestyle, but also to demonstrate it. This is very different from how the world sees leadership. A popular contemporary view is that a person's public office can be separated from his private life and the two do not have to go together to qualify for office or responsibility. A recent TV programme on J. F. Kennedy considered some of the secrets of his leadership. It emphasized positive aspects: he was organized and purposeful; open to ideas from every quarter; impassioned in speech; warm and accessible to people; assiduous in training and preparation; fearless in going to the source of a problem; capable of bringing out the best in those who worked with him; and ruthlessly analytical of difficulties and challenges. But these good qualities were then seriously undermined by a sad feature of his leadership: his personal life was not a good example to people and moral misdemeanours were covered up. A prime responsibility of leaders is to be examples so that even when they are dead their influence continues and their example can be imitated (Hebrews 13:7).

The leader a servant

Christian leaders are to be servants. None would deny that the Lord Jesus Christ was the ideal and perfect leader, but his spirit and attitude were very different from what we commonly associate with leadership. He took upon him 'the very nature of a servant' and we are commanded to do the same (Philippians 2:5, 7). He washed the disciples' feet and told these leaders in training that in carrying out this act he was giving them an example of leadership (John 13:15). James and John aspired to leadership, although from wrong motives. The Lord Jesus did not decry their ambition but he showed them the channels through which such a desire had to flow. He called the disciples together and said, 'You know that the rulers of the Gentiles lord it over them, and their high officials exercise authority over them. Not so with you. Instead, whoever wants to become great among you must be your servant, and whoever wants to be first must be your slave — just as the Son of Man did not come to be served, but to serve, and to give his life as a ransom for many' (Matthew 20:25-28).

'Whoever wants to be first must be your slave' (20:27). These words show the amazing paradox of Christian leadership: to lead we must be servants. In other kinds of leadership, individuals may endeavour to build up spheres of personal power, but not so godly Christians. Tremendous self-restraint is necessary in Christian leadership, especially if we have been accustomed to exercising responsibility in secular spheres. Even as our Saviour's leadership involved the cross, so Christian leaders will know and accept the call to self-denial and sacrifice.

The leader a teacher

A further distinctive characteristic of Christian leadership must be mentioned: Christian leaders are intended always to be teachers. It would be an interesting study to enquire into the subsequent activities of those who worked both under and with the apostle Paul. Clearly he gave a lot of time to instructing them, as his letters to Timothy and Titus show. His direction to Timothy regarding a leadership succession is enlightening: 'And the things you have heard me say in the presence of many witnesses entrust to reliable men who will also be qualified to teach others' (2 Timothy 2:2).

Christian leaders must possess a sure grasp of Christian truth and the principles that are to govern the life and service of God's people. They should regard the instruction of other potential leaders — from the point of view of ensuring a godly succession — a major responsibility. They should not be those who greedily hold on to office or responsibility because of the pleasure it gives, but instead should desire that others may share the privilege of office with them. This is not a *natural* characteristic but it is a *spiritual* characteristic of those 'full of the Holy Spirit'.

While Christian leadership has many qualities in common with other kinds of leadership, it is, nevertheless, distinctive by reason of its major requirement that we should know experimentally the power of God's Spirit. From this distinguishing experience come most of the other distinctions to which we have drawn attention.

Prayer

Heavenly Father, please help me to see how essential the required qualities for spiritual leadership are. Recognizing that they are qualities that all Christians, whether leaders or not, should exhibit, help me by your gracious Spirit to become more like our Lord Jesus Christ and ever more obedient to him. For his name's sake. Amen.

Questions for Bible study groups

Read Matthew 20:20-28; John 13:1-17

1. What false views of leadership did the Lord Jesus correct in his response to the request of the mother of Zebedee's sons?
2. In what ways is the Lord Jesus an example to us in his leadership? Where does the power come from to follow his example?
3. How would you answer those who say that their personal life can be separated from their public life?

Questions for church leaders

1. *How can we test whether we are in leadership because we enjoy it or out of love for our Lord Jesus Christ and his people? Why is such testing appropriate?*
2. *How might fear of criticism hinder us from making right choices?*
3. *In what ways is our leadership energetic and enthusiastic, and in what ways is it not?*
4. *What will show that we are taking seriously God's requirement that we should be filled with the Holy Spirit?*

3.

Prescribed tests for leaders

The distinctive requirement of Christian leadership — that people should be filled with the Holy Spirit — means that if candidates lack this one qualification, although possessing many others, they should not be appointed.

As we suggested in the last chapter, questions immediately arise. How do we know if people are spiritually equipped for leadership? How are we able to recognize those who are filled with the Spirit? Paul anticipated such questions when he wrote to his assistants, Timothy and Titus, giving them instructions for the appointment of leaders in the churches. He knew that those whose lives are under the control of the Holy Spirit exhibit definable and recognizable characteristics so that there will be no doubt as to their spiritual readiness.

Basic passages

Acts 6:1-7; 1 Timothy 3:1-13; Titus 1:5-11; and 1 Peter 5:1-4 are the four New Testament passages that deal either directly or indirectly with tests for potential leaders. We may call them *prescribed* tests because Paul uses the word *must*: 'the overseer *must be*' (1 Timothy 3:2; Titus 1:7).

The correct procedure is not that a church should appoint spiritual leaders and then tell them what they ought to be like; that is putting the cart before the horse. Rather, a church is to identify those who are already fulfilling the qualifications and appoint them to office.

Seven questions

The prescribed tests established in the four Scripture passages may be presented in the form of seven questions. While the appointment of elders and deacons is particularly in view the principles behind the tests apply to every sphere of Christian leadership.

1. Do they have a good reputation?

This was one of the first questions asked in the early church (1 Timothy 3:7). Candidates for office were to be well spoken of, and recognized as those whose lives backed up what they professed (3:8). Our reputation is what the majority of people may say or think about us. Although they may be mistaken, the reputation we have is much more accurate than we may sometimes like to believe. Of the right sort of candidate for leadership, all Christians should be able to speak a good word.

A good reputation is not to be confined, however, to the Christian community. Paul's words in 1 Timothy 3:7 stress it must be recognized by 'outsiders'. Business associates, work colleagues or employers should be able to speak of Christians as both conscientious and reliable. Neighbours should be able to testify to Christians' good character and the ease with which they get on with them. If candidates for leadership do not have such a reputation, they should not be appointed, for such an

appointment could then encourage them to lead a double-life
— to all appearances, an exemplary life in the church, but a
sub-standard Christian life outside. The kind of people we are
in our daily work and home is essentially the kind of people,
and help, we are in the church.

2. Are they of blameless character?

No one justly expects potential leaders to be perfect; but people
have a right to expect that Christian leaders should be blameless:
that is to say, that their lives measure up to the standards set by
God in the Bible for the living of the Christian life. Potential
leaders should be tested to prove their blamelessness, even
as employers may put potential employees under a period
of probation before making their appointment permanent
(1 Timothy 3:10).

In every area of their life, leaders are to be 'above reproach'
(1 Timothy 3:2). Relationships with those of the other sex must
be exemplary; and in the marriage relationship, they must be
absolutely faithful (3:2, 12; Titus 1:6). No bad habits should
control them; they are to be in command of their lifestyle
(1 Timothy 3:3). This emphasis upon character is obviously
right. Character inspires confidence and is more important
than aptitude and proficiency. Peter, trained in leadership by the
Lord Jesus, knew that what was required to lead God's people
was the positive example of a life above reproach (1 Peter 5:3).
Even as our Saviour led by example (John 13:1-17), so should
his people's leaders do the same.

3. Is their life marked by self-control?

All disqualifying factors — quarrelsomeness (1 Timothy 3:3),
love of money (3:3), being overbearing and bossy (Titus 1:7),

insincerity (1 Timothy 3:8), a domineering spirit (1 Peter 5:3), drunkenness (1 Timothy 3:3, 8; Titus 1:7), violence (1 Timothy 3:3; Titus 1:7), and quick-temperedness (1:7) — spring from a lack of control over either ambitions, speech, temperament, or physical desires.

Like others, prospective leaders have to earn money to pay their way in life, but they should not be obsessed by the desire for material possessions (1 Timothy 3:3). They will have opinions to put forward, but they should not be so intent on having their own way that they pass over what other people think and say (Titus 1:7). The kindest people may get caught up unintentionally in an unhelpful argument but leaders are not to be controversialists. They should avoid disagreement or argument, providing no principle is compromised (1 Timothy 3:3). The tongue is where self-control is most urgent (3:2-3). Words later proved to have been insincere seriously undermine a good reputation.

The demands for vigilance, soberness and good behaviour (3:2-3) all serve to emphasize the priority of self-control (Titus 1:8). Under all circumstances, not least under provocation, leaders should be self-possessed and able to exercise restraint. They should not speak first and think afterwards; instead they should think first, and then speak; and sometimes decide not to speak at all. An ordered life characterized by courtesy and dignity, besides bringing credit to the gospel, is an essential qualification for Christian leadership.

4. Are they people of spiritual maturity?

Those recently converted are not eligible for leadership (1 Timothy 3:6). Quite apart from the spiritual responsibilities they are unable to fulfil, all are prone to the sin of conceit. For this reason beginners in the faith are not to be appointed to important offices since it may go to their head and they may bring judgement upon themselves, a judgement contrived by the devil. This is not to say that those recently converted are to be left idle; rather, they are to be given as many opportunities as possible for discovering their gifts and proving themselves (1 Timothy 3:10).

Leaders are to be treading the pathway of holiness (Titus 1:8). If they are to lead others on in the Christian life, they must be examples of commitment to the Lord Jesus Christ and of practical godliness. They need to have mature judgement so that they discern what is good and follow it, and what is evil and forsake it — in other words, those who love what is good (1:8). Maturity is the product of a growing understanding of and obedience to God's will as it is revealed in the Scriptures. Maturity, although a daily process, does not happen in a moment.

If spiritual leaders are to be 'able to teach' (1 Timothy 3:2), they need to be well taught in the Word of God and eager to improve their knowledge. The mystery of the faith is to be held 'with a clear conscience' (3:9); a firm hold on the deep truths and doctrines of the Christian faith is vital. Besides living in obedience to the Scriptures, they have to be able to encourage others and refute error by God's Word (Titus 1:9). A primary responsibility of Christian leadership is to feed and nurture the flock (1 Peter 5:2).

The stability that comes from spiritual maturity is vital. Paul described the early leaders of the church — Peter, James and John — as 'pillars' of the church (Galatians 2:9). Spiritual maturity is necessary for such a description to be true of those called to leadership.

5. Is their home life well ordered?

Leaders should manage their home life well and, if married, win obedience from their children. Those unable to manage their own family cannot expect to be successful in looking after a congregation of God's people (1 Timothy 3:5). If they say, 'We cannot sometimes get to church as a family on a Sunday because we are just not organized,' they should not be thought suitable for spiritual leadership. If they allow their children to hinder them playing their part in the life and witness of the church — not that they should fall short of aiming at being the best parents possible — they are not in a position to be called to leadership.

Rather than hindering a parent's good name, children are to enhance it (3:12). Potential leaders' children should be believers, and not open to the charge of being disobedient or disrespectful. The success parents have in their homes is often an indication of the help they may give in the church. Some qualification is needed here. Experience shows that the godliest people, who may be eminently suited for leadership, can have children who grow up to be unbelievers. This test, therefore, needs to be applied with sensitivity and wisdom. Nevertheless, it needs to be seriously considered.

Over the years potential leaders have raised with me a number of times Paul's statement in Titus 1:6 that, besides being blameless and having a right marriage relationship, a spiritual leader's children must believe and not be 'open to the charge of being wild and disobedient'. Commentaries make the point that the word translated *believe* may carry the meaning of 'faithful' as it has sometimes been translated. Matthew Henry interestingly interprets the AV translation *having faithful children* as meaning that they are 'obedient and good, brought up in the true Christian faith, and living according to it, at least as far as the endeavours of the parents can avail'. In other words, the phrase *whose children believe* is parallel with 1 Timothy 3:4 ('he must manage his own family well and see that his children obey him with proper respect') implying that *faithful children* are *obedient and respectful children.* If people's suitability is in doubt because of the requirements expressed in Paul's words, my inclination is to suggest that the individuals concerned should share their personal situation and circumstances with those who are already in church leadership, asking for their prayers, and then their considered and honest convictions in the light of their understanding and interpretation of the Scriptures. Where we cannot be absolutely sure that our interpretation is right, there is blessing and direction when those who share and consider such issues can say, 'It seems good to us and the Holy Spirit.'

A home has to be well ordered if it is to provide hospitality effectively and at the same time commend the gospel. Where possible, Christian leaders are to be outstanding in this area of kindness (3:2). To have an open home implies that the life in the home is in such harmony with the faith we profess that all its communal life may be open to view — at a moment's notice — without embarrassment. If ever people have the opportunity of seeing us in our homes their opinion of us is influenced by what they see there more than anywhere else, and with good reason.

6. *If married, are husband and wife at one in the Christian faith?*

Everything we have established up until this point requires that a husband and wife should be united in their profession of the

Christian faith and their desire to live for our Lord Jesus Christ.
If this is not the case, it will be difficult to organize the home in
accordance with Christian principles, not least in the spiritual
education of children. The latter rests in practice more upon
the wife than upon the husband, although it ought to be a
shared responsibility.

Although hospitality can be given where husband and wife
are not one in the faith, it will not be the Christian fellowship
that constitutes the particular helpfulness of Christian
hospitality. The coming of Christians into the home to share
their experience of Christ could emphasize the unhappy division
between husband and wife.

A wife's spiritual preparedness is as important as her husband's
(3:11). When a man is appointed to leadership in the church,
besides expecting much of him, people will tend to expect
much of the wife, sometimes unreasonably. If their spiritual
relationship with the Lord Jesus Christ is right, husband and
wife will not find this irksome but will be united in their
desire to expend themselves and their home in God's service.
Husbands and wives can be a tremendous help to one another
in the responsibilities they exercise — and a great hindrance.
Those who aspire after responsibility in the church should
be those who make their marriage partner's spiritual welfare
a major concern. If they do not do so, how can they express
an honest concern for the spiritual well-being of the church?
Spiritual concern begins at home.

7. Do they already give of themselves willingly to God's people?

Potential leaders are to be doing many of these things already
and demonstrating these characteristics before ever they are
called to leadership rather than, as suggested earlier, being

appointed, and then exhorted to attain them. We do not give hospitality simply because we are commanded to do so, but because the desire is in our heart already. Likewise those who are apt to teach, because they feel so strongly about the truth, feel compelled to communicate it. True undershepherds reveal themselves as such without being officially appointed to office, and people go to them as a matter of course when they want spiritual help.

Leadership is demanding in that there are no limits to what may be expected. Leaders' time is not their own; their leisure is often interrupted; their willingness to sacrifice is constantly tested. If, in the capacity in which they are already serving, they give grudging and half-hearted service, they should not be considered for leadership.

Spiritual qualities are priorities

These prescribed tests for leaders are ignored at peril. The weakness and ineffectiveness of many a group of Christians may be traced to failure at this point. Significantly, no reference in the Bible is made either to intellectual ability or social status. Spiritual qualities are the priorities. As we think of our previous chapter, these spiritual qualities are the evidence and proof of the Spirit's presence and control in a Christian's life. They can be true only as the experience of being filled with the Spirit is known.

These tests — which are to be applied to all possible candidates for leadership — reflect the standards God sets for every Christian's life. Christian leaders differ from non-leaders not so much in kind as in degree.

Prayer

Almighty God, Heavenly Father, as I consider the essential qualifications for leadership I cannot but be overwhelmed by a sense of the seemingly impossible standards required. Help me to recognize that they are meant to humble me and to underline my dependence upon you and the grace and strength of our Lord Jesus. Grant that all Christians, and not least those whom you are calling to leadership, will be challenged to strive after holiness and Christlikeness. This I ask for our Lord Jesus Christ's sake. Amen.

Questions for Bible study groups

Read 1 Timothy 3:1-13; Titus 1:5-11; 1 Peter 5:1-4.

1. What do these three passages have in common?
2. How different are these qualifications for Christian leadership from the expectations of our contemporary world of its leaders?
3. What are the most difficult qualifications to fulfil and why?
4. How seriously do you feel your church fellowship takes these requirements?

Questions for church leaders

1. *Good reputation, blamelessness, self-control, spiritual maturity, a well-ordered home, marital spiritual oneness and*

harmony and wholehearted service: what will it mean to examine ourselves in these areas?

2. *Which of these qualifications and requirements do we find the most challenging and how can we help one another in their achievement?*

3. *When we appoint people to positions of leadership do we present these standards to the church? How is it best done?*

4.

Discovering your potential

A basic assumption behind this book is the conviction that many Christians have ability for leadership that is hidden both to themselves and to others. We need some guidance as to the manner in which such potential may be recognized.

Church fellowship

It is important to state the obvious here. We must begin by identifying ourselves fully with the company of God's people to which we belong. As we work with them, our gifts — both natural and spiritual — will come to light, often without our seeking or realizing it. We will never, for example, be in a position to lead others effectively if we have not first learned to work successfully with others.

One thing inevitably leads to another in leadership, as in most spheres. Stephen, whose story is recorded in Acts 6 and 7, became known through his involvement with the church in Jerusalem as a man who was full of wisdom and of the Spirit. He clearly functioned as a healthy member of the body of Christ.

This led to his appointment to office for the care and well-being of others. But it did not stop there. He then displayed evangelistic gifts and the ability to give leadership to the church. If we are only on the fringe of the life of our local church, our first priority must be to become more fully involved in its life and work.

Prayer

The attitude in which we seek to discover leadership potential must be that of prayer. Conceit and pride can spring up quickly and spoil us if we are not watchful. To consider the whole matter prayerfully is an important safeguard. If we have any thoughts about our possible leadership potential, we should ask God to show us what our potential is and, perhaps better still, show it to others.

The Scriptures encourage us to seek understanding from God as to our best usefulness. While we are not to cherish exaggerated views of our abilities, we are encouraged to think our way to a sober estimate of them (Romans 12:3). In our fear of thinking too highly of ourselves, we may foolishly go to the other extreme of not thinking at all! The concern to be our best and to develop our gifts in the interests of our Saviour's kingdom is not contrary to humility.

God gives us faith in ourselves — in a way that is consistent with humility — when we submit ourselves to his direction for service. It is not a faith in what we can do on our own, but a confidence as to what we may do with his help. Such a confidence develops and grows as we ask for his help and place before him our hopes, ambitions, fears and doubts.

Stability

Clearly, our potential has much to do with whether or not we match up to the prescribed tests for leaders outlined in the previous chapter.

A major hindrance to the exercise of leadership is instability arising from lack of self-control. It is not sufficient to be an *occasional* example to believers in speech and behaviour, but it is necessary to be a *consistent* example (1 Timothy 4:12). Moments of instability and the unhelpful example they give often cause others to stumble. The apostle Peter knew this personally; and he learnt bitter lessons as a result. Having given a positive lead to the Christians in Galatia, he later led them astray through a moment of moral cowardice (Galatians 2:11-14). Fortunately, for our encouragement, Peter's failure did not disqualify him from leadership; but his lapse points to the importance of dependability.

We should examine our stability. We may best do so by considering first our reliability in getting a job finished once we begin. Then we should determine the extent to which we allow our moods and feelings to hinder us performing tasks assigned to us. Next, we should review the control we have over the expression of our feelings, especially when we are under pressure. Finally, and by no means least important, we should consider the 'aliveness' and stability of our fellowship with God.

Prayerful self-examination reveals areas of life where we most easily lose our self-control. Circumstances and situations will spring to mind that are a recurring problem for us. To be forewarned is to be forearmed. We should consider how we may avoid repeating mistakes, and ask for God's help to avoid obvious pitfalls. Positive action in these areas is part of leadership potential.

Past circumstances

No one becomes a leader in a moment; everything we have done in the past influences what we now do and what we will do in the future. Gifts of leadership may often be apparent in childhood. It will be helpful to think back over our whole life and see if there have been circumstances when in the absence of leadership, we have assumed it quite naturally or have shown some love of it. Have we looked at situations requiring change and leadership and simply longed to be able to take some initiative? Have people looked to us, almost automatically, when they have needed or wanted a lead in a particular matter? Do we find it easy to carry people along with us in what we feel needs to be done? Questions such as these will provide affirmative answers if we have leadership potential.

Readiness to take the initiative

Everyday situations provide scope for initiative. Though there are always jobs needing to be done and people available to do them, more often than not, the tasks remain unaccomplished because no one takes the initiative but leaves the work to someone else. The potential leader finds it easy to be resourceful and enterprising. Throughout the Gospel narratives Peter comes to the fore most often as the leader among the Twelve. Even when overwhelmed by his failure to remain steadfast at the time of Jesus' betrayal, Peter continued as leader (John 21:1-3; Acts 2:14).

Do we take the initiative when no one else does? This question is relevant to both great and small situations. Let us imagine one such minor circumstance. We arrive one evening at the church hall for a meeting. We find three or four other people there already, somewhat at a loss because through some oversight the hall is not laid out properly for the meeting. What would we do? Would we simply stand with them and regret the situation? Alternatively, would we set about arranging the hall ourself? Or would we suggest to the others that we arrange things *together*, indicating the way in which it should be done? To do nothing or to do it all on our own would show little initiative. Little incidents like this reveal leadership potential.

Often when Christians discuss major issues they may quickly agree as to their urgency but may lack the initiative to suggest constructive measures, with the result that even after much discussion a meeting closes with no satisfactory conclusion. At such times, do we find ourselves deliberately striving to ensure that positive action, however small, comes out of the discussion? If so, we demonstrate a measure of leadership potential.

Concern for people

Christian leadership is different from other forms of leadership because it has as its *ruling* principle the well-being and service of those who are led. The emblem of Christian leadership, derived from the washing of the disciples' feet by the Lord Jesus Christ (John 13:1-16), is a basin of water and a towel.

In some spheres individuals may lead without a genuine concern for people. They may even be indifferent to the best interests of those for whom they are responsible. However, because of the priority of love (1 Corinthians 13), Christian leaders are required to have a concern and interest in people and especially for those whom they lead.

If we withdraw into our shell and expect other people to take the initiative, perhaps in raising some vexing issue, we will not make a leader. When we see individuals getting among people, identifying with them and getting alongside them — and not just those who are of their particular type — we probably see individuals with a capacity for leadership. Christian leaders must love people: they should enjoy meeting them and bringing out their best.

To discover our potential we should examine honestly the way in which we get along with others and the concern we feel for them. If we withdraw from contact with people, feeling unable to give of ourselves freely to them, we have identified a serious hindrance to leadership.

Potential leaders should possess an interest in people for their own sakes. This concern will be seen in endeavouring to be as approachable as possible and in showing friendship. Our interest will not be out of curiosity but because of a genuine concern for people's well-being. We have all met people who are willing to talk about themselves and their circumstances but who become quite vacant and disinterested when it comes to listening to our needs and difficulties: such people are not qualified for leadership.

Ability to administrate

Administration is a distinguishable gift from leadership but every leader must to some extent be an administrator. This is not to imply that all leaders enjoy spending time organizing and establishing methods for keeping things in order. However, they recognize that careful organization and attention to detail are necessary if projects and initiatives are to be carried forward harmoniously, without friction. Hopefully, leaders will be supported in the exercise of their gift by administrators, but they themselves can never opt out of the responsibility of seeing that things are done decently and in order. If they are not careful in this area many of their best efforts will be fruitless.

Readiness to assume responsibility

Potential leaders do not have to be prodded and pushed all the time to do a task to which they have committed themselves. Part of the 'proving' of leadership potential is the testing of our willingness to take on and carry out responsibility.

When the time arrives for the allocation of tasks, it is possible to shrink from becoming too much involved, and to find excuses that provide an escape from commitment. Clearly, when they know that it is the right thing for them, leaders should never shirk taking responsibility.

While all of us should fear over-commitment, potential leaders do not ask to be excused when legitimate responsibility is offered. Recognizing that our plans and personal programme may be frequently disrupted we will happily accept the implications without complaining about the load that is put upon us. Those who make a fuss about what is their duty — but enjoy it nevertheless — spoil their potential.

Our present preparedness to assume responsibility is probably seen most accurately in our past readiness to shoulder it. The reliability of our present intentions is best proved by our past performance. If we have been unafraid of responsibility up until now and have tried to equip ourselves for its discharge as it has been placed upon us, then we may regard ourselves as ready for further responsibility.

Time to give

Leadership is costly in time. Time has to be given to planning and organization; time must be given to individuals; time ought to be given to the instruction of others in the tasks delegated to them; time is required to learn as much as possible about more effective leadership.

If we are interested in discovering our potential we should ask ourselves whether we are both willing and able to give the time that is necessary. Leaders do not have set hours to do their work. At any moment, they have to be willing to deal with emergencies or to give time to a project presented to them. Without warning, someone may arrive expecting guidance and help. If we want to be able to call our time our own and to regulate our life to our personal convenience and satisfaction, we ought not to contemplate leadership.

Use of present opportunities

The more we have, the more God gives us. This scriptural principle is similar to another: the Christian who is faithful in little is given responsibility over much. Both statements emphasize that God calls no one to leadership without there having been faithfulness in earlier, and probably much smaller, responsibilities.

All of us are given opportunities to serve and to take the lead when circumstances demand it. Because the opportunities may seem small and humdrum, we may make the mistake of imagining that they are unimportant; but, in fact, nothing is unimportant. The faithful discharge of present duties is a most accurate indication of leadership potential. Leaders do not become faithful in the discharge of their duties simply because they are called 'leaders'; they are faithful because they have a desire to be faithful to God, whether he calls them to leadership or obscurity.

Our use of present opportunities fashions us for the discharge of those we may have in the future. I recall a powerful example of this. I heard a young man give an extremely competent presentation on an important issue to a church meeting. I suddenly realized that both his ability to speak in a public meeting and to put his thoughts together had been developed and honed through his serving on the committee of the young people's meeting. Present opportunities for service and initiative that are missed may rule out the seizing of future opportunities.

Conviction of others

If we feel God may be calling us to prepare ourselves for leadership and that we have potential that needs to be released and put to good use, we should not neglect the importance of the opinion of spiritually mature Christians who know us well.

It may be appropriate to ask the opinion and advice of our spiritual leaders. As they pray and discuss the matter together, wanting to know God's will, we may depend upon the Holy Spirit to guide them to a conviction that will either confirm or contradict our own. If they point out some weakness or potential disqualification, we should not resent it but endeavour with God's help to remedy it, thankful for their honesty and care of us.

Willingness to learn

Essential to discovering our potential for leadership is our willingness to learn. In many spheres of life, some form of apprenticeship is available, alongside perhaps more formal instruction in a task. More often than not we will feel that we learn most through the apprenticeship, especially if we are humble enough to recognize that we have everything to learn. We learn most when good example and instruction go together. Such experience will enhance our convictions about God's will for our life and fuel our expectations.

Basic to discovering our potential is our willingness, desire and determination to learn from others. When a task is committed to us, we should not hesitate to ask those who entrust it to us how it should be done. We should jump at the opportunity of an 'apprenticeship' to those who exercise leadership, then carefully observe how they go about it and ask questions, even if we feel our questions display regrettable ignorance.

Basic questions

We began this chapter by emphasizing the priority of prayer in discovering potential. With that firmly established, various questions have emerged that we should be willing to ask ourselves — and to have others ask of us too.

May I suggest that you ask yourself the following questions in an attitude of prayer before God?

- Are you stable in your character and Christian profession?
- Have you found yourself taking the lead when working with others?
- Do you take the initiative when no one else does?
- Have you an obvious concern for people?
- Do you rise to responsibility?
- Are you willing to give time to leadership?
- Are you using to the full your present opportunities of service and responsibility?
- Are you quick to learn and to accept advice?
- Would those who know you well recommend you for leadership?

Negative answers to some of these questions do not mean that you have no leadership potential; they may mean that there are areas in your life that need 'tidying up' before you can go any further. If that is so, aim to give attention to them immediately.

If, however, these considerations appear to rule out leadership potential, do not be discouraged. The New Testament speaks of the human body as an illustration of the church of Christ. Not all parts of the human body have an equally conspicuous part to play, but they are all just as necessary. Some of the inconspicuous components of the body are more important than those that are prominent. Although leaders are important, they are by no means more important in their function than less conspicuous Christians in theirs. The most important place for us all in the church of Christ, and in the local church in particular, is the place *God* has appointed for us.

Prayer

Lord, I am afraid of my pride and of being presumptuous. Help me by your Spirit not to think too highly of myself and at the same time neither to doubt nor put aside any calling that you may be giving me to serve you and your people in the body of Christ. May my will only be to do your will. For Jesus Christ's sake. Amen.

Questions for Bible study groups

Read Romans 12:1-8

1. *Romans 12:1-3:* What are the important steps in discovering God's will and what should be our principal motive in wanting to make that discovery?
2. *Romans 12:4-8*: What do these verses teach us about spiritual gifts?
3. What is the particular responsibility of those whose gift is leadership? What does this mean in practice?
4. Looking back upon your own experience, how has one responsibility in service led to another?

Questions for church leaders

1. *In what ways are we providing opportunities for our members to discover their leadership potential? How are we encouraging them to do so?*

2. *What time do we give in our leadership meetings to discussing the emerging gifts of leadership within the church?*
3. *In what ways can we provide and encourage spiritual apprenticeships?*
4. *How can we encourage people to prayerfully consider their best contribution to the church fellowship?*

5.

The recognition of leaders and their training

Leadership potential has to be brought into action so that it may be recognized. Latent skills and abilities need to be developed and put to good use. While the apostles became the men of God that they were through the power and grace of our Lord Jesus Christ, he undoubtedly knew their hidden promise when he first called them. There was nothing haphazard in his choice; and for three years he gave himself to training them and developing their potential.

Identifying potential

The first stage in the process is identifying those who have leadership potential.

Convictions given by the Spirit to others

They may be recognized by clear and definite convictions the Holy Spirit gives to others — and especially to the church leadership — about their gifts and calling. Paul writes, 'Timothy, my son, I give you this instruction in keeping with the prophecies once made about you, so that by following them you may fight the good fight' (1 Timothy 1:18). We are given no indications as to what these prophetic predictions were. Probably they were convictions given to Paul and other Christian leaders concerning Timothy's gifts and future work, something similar to what happened with Paul and Barnabas in the church at Antioch (Acts 13:1-3).

Imagine an elders' or leaders' meeting, where specific needs are under discussion and the spiritual growth of individual members is the leaders' concern. Someone may say, 'I have a conviction that John has a gift for pastoral ministry.' 'I agree,' responds another. And then all present spontaneously declare, 'The same thought has come to me.' 'We ought to encourage him deliberately then in this direction, and equip him,' suggests one of the elders. In this way the Holy Spirit gives a common mind about the future usefulness of an individual, and that insight leads to the recognition of a potential leader.

Humble aspirations for leadership

Potential leaders are often recognized by humble aspirations they have for spiritual leadership. Paul writes, 'Here is a trustworthy saying: If anyone sets his heart on being an overseer, he desires a noble task' (1 Timothy 3:1). Such a desire, of course, can be proud, selfish and unworthy. But the Holy Spirit directs those whom he chooses for leadership by giving them leanings in that direction. For example, some will be finding particular enjoyment in exercising spiritual care for others. People will go to them with their problems and spiritual concerns with ease and confidence. This will inevitably come to the notice of the leaders of the church fellowship. Leaders will then say to them, 'We're glad to see this concern you have, and the way in which God is using you.' Their response will reveal their delight in such opportunities of serving God and his people. Once more, potential leaders have been unearthed, and should then be encouraged, equipped and trained.

Aptness to teach

Potential leaders are to be recognized by their aptness to teach (1 Timothy 3:2). People look for instruction to those who are able to teach; they recognize their judgement to be sound because they consistently turn them with profit to the Scriptures. They do not have to be public speakers. Rather, they may be private instructors and encouragers from God's Word. They gradually stand out as potential leaders because they are reliable and qualified to teach others (2 Timothy 2:2). They should then be given every encouragement to take seriously the task of faithfully transmitting God's truth to others, and caring for them in the faith.

Establishing teachers' and preachers' classes, no matter how small the number of people involved, has a contribution here as also does recommending distance learning courses to increase knowledge and understanding of the Bible.

Basic qualifications

The second stage is to see if the basic qualifications for leadership, established in chapter 3, are being met, and, if not, to bring them to the attention of individuals. Where these basic qualifications are present, together with the recognizable signs of potential leadership, training may begin. Where, however, these qualifications are absent, the matter should be taken up with the people concerned and discussed honestly, frankly and sensitively. Where there is true potential — the Holy Spirit's gift — there will be a willingness to put things in order. This duty of frank speaking should not be neglected. It is not easy, but it is essential.

Training

The third stage is to determine how such potential leaders should be trained.

Careful instruction

First, they require careful instruction from established leaders. Barnabas taught Paul. Paul taught Timothy. Timothy was to teach reliable men. They in turn were to teach others (2:2). That is how the process has gone on until today. We all need examples upon which to model our lives. Timothy needed Paul's example, and it must have been a continuing role model and inspiration to Timothy: 'You ... know all about my teaching, my way of life, my purpose, faith, patience, love, endurance, persecutions, sufferings — what kinds of things happened to me in Antioch, Iconium and Lystra, the persecutions I endured,' Paul wrote to him. 'Yet the Lord rescued me from all of them' (2 Timothy 3:10-11).

Established leaders should recognize their responsibility for training and equipping others. An essential quality of leadership is the ability to equip others to lead. We must ask ourselves whether or not we are seriously engaged in this task.

Instruction from Scripture

Secondly, potential leaders are to be trained by deliberate instruction from the Scriptures concerning their tasks. In his letters to Timothy and Titus Paul provides detailed instruction about the exercise of leadership in the church of God.

Just as potential leaders are best trained by means of the deliberate study of the Scriptures on leadership, there is also a place for bringing biblical teaching on the subject before the local church. As suggested we can use the letters to Timothy or Titus. Or it can be done through a study of our Lord's teaching, or consideration of biblical examples of leadership.

Individual instruction

Thirdly, potential leaders are best trained on an individual basis. Much training can be done in a group. But there also needs to be a close relationship between an established leader and people who are concerned to equip themselves. It is significant that Paul wrote *personal* letters to Timothy and Titus. The essential instruction he gives about church order, for example, is identical. But the temperament and disposition of these men was different. Paul needed to counsel Timothy about his timidity, his youthful appearance and the state of his stomach (1 Timothy 5:23)! If people are to be trained for leadership, they must want constructive criticism, and be willing to accept it — and principally from the person to whom they look for an example.

Opportunity for testing

Fourthly, opportunities must be provided for the testing and proving of potential leaders. Writing of deacons, Paul says,

'They must first be tested; and then if there is nothing against them, let them serve as deacons' (1 Timothy 3:10). The word 'tested' means to prove or examine, and was used of testing the genuineness of metals. Various tasks should be entrusted to potential leaders to see how well they carry them out, and how they get on with people. The deliberate appointment of 'deputies' gives rise to greater opportunities for people to be tested. Their 'directability' should be checked. (Paul's instructions to Timothy in 2 Timothy 4:9-22 show that he anticipated Timothy being directable in his service for God.)

Establish a syllabus of instruction

The fourth stage is establishing a syllabus of instruction. In introducing this syllabus it ought to be explained that all leadership in the church of Christ is to be spiritual and pastoral, much as practical and organizational skills need to be encouraged. God's concern is for people, and for the eternal well-being of their souls. This concern is to be shared by his people, and leaders are raised up to fulfil the implications of it. (A suggested syllabus of instruction based upon 1 and 2 Timothy is to be found at the end of this chapter.)

Training potential leaders is no light assignment

Paul took the training of others seriously and persevered with it. Being a leader is no easy task. There are many temptations both to give up and to lower standards. Think of what Paul had to say to Timothy to keep him at his assignment. He urged him to stay on in Ephesus (1 Timothy 1:3). He instructed him to be inspired by convictions voiced by others concerning his call (1:18). He charged him to bear in mind the coming again of the Lord Jesus and the account we all must render then (6:14; 2 Timothy 4:1). Because spiritual leaders are so essential to the body of Christ, the devil — not surprisingly — makes them a special object of attack.

The reminder of the picture of the body of Christ brings us to a final point which provides balance. *Leaders are essential to the body of Christ but in the sight and purpose of God they are not more important than other members of the body.* Each and every member is vital. The prime objective is not to be a leader, but to be in our God-appointed place in the body. And, at the same time, it must be said, quoting from the New English Bible translation of 1 Timothy 3:1, 'To aspire to leadership is an honourable ambition.'

Guidelines for potential leaders

- Make sure you are in fellowship and good standing in a local church where your gifts and abilities can be observed and confirmed.
- Equip yourself for leadership in every way open to you.
- Try to identify your weaknesses, enlisting the help of your friends, and, if you are married, your marriage partner most of all; and determine how to correct and overcome them.
- Strive hard to learn from the example of others.
- Give of your best now in whatever tasks and responsibilities you have.
- Make it your priority to grow in the knowledge of our Lord and Saviour Jesus Christ.

A suggested syllabus of instruction based upon 1 and 2 Timothy

1. Priorities in spiritual responsibility

a. Public reading of the Scriptures (1 Timothy 4:13).
b. Preaching (4:13).
c. Teaching (4:13).
d. Righteousness (2 Timothy 2:22).
e. Faith (2:22).
f. Love (2:22).
g. Peace (2:22).
h. The avoidance of obvious perils: e.g. the desire for material wealth (1 Timothy 6:6-11), and association with those who use religion as a facade for underhand dealings and activities (2 Timothy 3:5).
(These subjects are the substance of pastoral theology.)

2. The nature of the spiritual conflict in which we are engaged and the principles to govern our warfare

a. How to wage a good warfare (1 Timothy 1:18), and to fight the good fight of faith (1 Timothy 6:12).

3. The importance of holding on to the faith and the truth

a. What it means to hold on to faith (1 Timothy 1:19).
b. The basic truths of the faith (e.g. 1 Timothy 1:15; 2:5-6; 2 Timothy 2:11-13; Titus 3:4-8).
c. How to be a workman who does not need to be ashamed, who correctly handles the word of truth (2 Timothy 2:15).
d. The use and profitability of applying the Word to every task and situation (2 Timothy 3:16-17).

e. Methods to be used in teaching others God's Word (1 Timothy 3:2).
(We are talking here of biblical and systematic theology.)

4. The place and priority of a good conscience

a. What is meant by a good conscience, and the perils of neglecting its priority (1 Timothy 1:19).
b. The kind of things which have to be watched if a good conscience is to be maintained (2 Timothy 2:20-22).
(We are talking here of experimental theology.)

5. The priority of prayer

a. Its various forms (1 Timothy 2:1).
b. Its scope (1 Timothy 2:2-4).
c. Its purpose (1 Timothy 2:2-4).
d. Its conditions (1 Timothy 2:8).

6. The standards of behaviour required of spiritual leaders (1 Timothy 3:1-13; Titus 1:5-9)

a. A good reputation (Acts 6:3; 1 Timothy 3:7-8).
b. A blameless character (1 Timothy 3:2-3, 10, 12; Titus 1:6; 1 Peter 5:3).
c. A life marked by self-control (1 Timothy 3:2-3, 8; Titus 1:7).
d. A growing spiritual maturity (1 Timothy 3:2, 6, 9-10; Titus 1:8; 1 Peter 5:2).
e. A well-ordered home and family life (1 Timothy 3:2, 5).
f. A willingness to give oneself freely to God's people (1 Timothy 3:1-13).
g. An example in speech and conduct, and of love, faith and purity (1 Timothy 4:12).

h. Consistency of example (2 Timothy 4:5).

7. **The instruction to be given to God's people systematically, regularly and thoroughly** (1 Timothy 4:6, 11; 5:7; 2 Timothy 2:14)

a. The pattern of sound teaching to be delivered to God's people (2 Timothy 1:13; cf. 1 Corinthians 15:1-8; 1 Thessalonians 4:1-8).
b. For example, the instruction to be given to Christians in different situations such as their daily employment (1 Timothy 6:1-2) and their attitude to wealth and its acquisition (6:17-19).
c. The spiritual truths which are to be continually presented to God's people as a challenge to better things (2 Timothy 2:14; cf. 2:11-13).

8. **The church order which is pleasing to God**

a. The place of women in the church (1 Timothy 2:9-15).
b. The behaviour which is appropriate in God's household (1 Timothy 3:15), between different ages (1 Timothy 5:1), and between the sexes (1 Timothy 5:2).
c. The procedure for calling men to hold office (1 Timothy 3:1-15; 5:22).
d. The handling of problems of church discipline (1 Timothy 5:19-21).

9. **The requirements of pastoral work** (2 Timothy 2:24-25)

a. The avoidance of quarrels.
b. Kindness.

c. Aptness and readiness to teach.
d. Patience and forbearance.
e. The correction of opponents with gentleness.
f. The ways in which God may be expected to work in people's lives as we work with him (2 Timothy 2:25-26; 3:8-9).
g. The use of the Scriptures in pastoral work: in correcting, rebuking, encouraging and teaching (2 Timothy 4:2).

10. Doing the work of an evangelist (2 Timothy 4:5)

a. How God works in conversion and regeneration.
b. What we can do.
c. What we cannot do.
d. What to look for in people's lives when they are showing an interest in the gospel.

11. Avoiding the perils of leadership

a. A peril of leadership is conceitedness leading to falling under the same judgement as the devil (1 Timothy 3:6).
b. The importance of self-watchfulness (1 Timothy 4:16).
c. The discipline required is like that of the soldier, the athlete and the farmer (2 Timothy 2:3-6).

12. What the future may hold

a. The sufferings which spiritual leaders may have to bear (2 Timothy 1:8; 2:3, 8-9; 3:12; 4:5).
b. The way things will work out in the last days (1 Timothy 4:1; 2 Timothy 3:1-9, 13) and the problems these events will provide for the church (2 Timothy 4:3-4).

13. **The duty and task of giving rise to further leaders** (2 Timothy 2:2)

a. Recognizing reliable men.
b. Teaching such men.
c. Working oneself out of a job.

14. **The secret of our strength**

a. The presence of the invisible Lord with us as we do his will (2 Timothy 4:17).
b. The Spirit given to us: of power, love and of self-discipline (2 Timothy 1:7).

Prayer

O Lord Jesus Christ, who has created and redeemed me, and has brought me to that which now I am; you know what you would do with me: do with me according to your will, for your tender mercy's sake. Amen.

A prayer of King Henry VI

Questions for Bible study groups

Read 2 Timothy 2:1-26; 3:10-11

1. Look carefully at 2 Timothy 2:2. What qualities was Timothy to look for in his recognition of potential leaders? How would you expect to recognize them?

2. *2 Timothy 2:1-13*: Paul uses three pictures to describe the demanding nature of Christian leadership. Which of these is the most meaningful to you and why?

3. *2 Timothy 2:8*: Why was it important for Paul to remind Timothy of Jesus Christ and his resurrection?

4. *2 Timothy 2:10*: Paul shares with Timothy his whole philosophy of Christian leadership and service. How would you explain these words to a new Christian?

5. How attractive to your church membership would a leadership course be — based, for example, on the suggested syllabus in this chapter?

Questions for church leaders

1. *What initiative do we take in identifying potential leaders?*

2. *How are we helping people who are apt to teach within the church fellowship to develop their gift?*

3. *What tasks are we entrusting to people with a view to testing their potential?*

4. *Should we establish a training course?*

6.
Basic practice

From this point on, we are going to imagine that you are in a position of leadership and that you value practical instruction to help you fulfil your responsibilities.

In this chapter, much of what we have to say about the practice of leadership may be summed up in the common expression 'know-how'. Those who are led expect their leaders to possess it; the belief that they do is one of the reasons why they follow them. To practise leadership effectively there are priorities we must understand and implement.

Know what is expected of you

You should aim at having as clear a conception as possible of exactly what is required of you in your particular position. First, try to establish thoughtfully and prayerfully what God requires from you; for if he has called you, there are specific purposes in your call, and you need to know them in so far as God chooses to reveal them.

If your position of responsibility is one mentioned in the Bible, learn God's requirements from it. Do not do this in a quick and cursory fashion, but rather with a careful determination to relate its principles to your situation.

Know what is expected of you from those whom you lead. They may not be slow in telling you, especially if you fall short of their expectations! It is important that before such a situation arises you should have worked out what kind of leadership they are looking to you to provide. Remember, however, that the leadership they want may not be the leadership they need and your task is to provide the latter. Do not follow the advice that a Bishop of Norwich was given by his predecessor, 'Welcome to Norfolk. If you want to lead someone in this part of the world, find out where they're going. And walk in front of them.'[1]

If you are to share leadership with others, make certain you are clear as to what your fellow leaders anticipate from you. See clearly where and how your responsibility fits in with theirs. Try to put yourself in their position so that you may appreciate their expectations.

Bad personal relationships come about through leaders going beyond the bounds of the responsibility entrusted to them, perhaps through excessive enthusiasm or indiscretion. These mistakes may be avoided if you understand what is rightly expected and keep to those bounds.

Know your people

An accomplished commanding officer of the 9th Argylls was Colonel James Clark, C.B. Not only did he command the battalion by virtue of his position but also by the admiration, loyalty and respect of every officer and man. The reason was not far to seek: 'Clark, in fact, was deeply and personally concerned with the welfare of every man in the battalion, and the men knew it. By that strange gift, which marks a great headmaster, he knew most of them by name. That was the secret of his power over them. They would have followed him anywhere.'[2]

Getting to know people comes more readily to some than to others; if it comes with difficulty to you then greater effort will be necessary, but it is worthwhile. Not only know by name those whom you lead but, where possible, try to have a fair estimate of what may be reasonably expected of each one. Recognize that people have different potential or contributions to make, and will require varying forms of encouragement, recognition and reward.

Know what has to be done

You, if no one else, need to have an overall picture of the work in which you are involved; to grasp the relationship of the individual to the whole; and to see how small details fit into the big picture. Aim to have good knowledge of the task before you, and a measure of confidence with regard to it. This is true whether you are an elder or a deacon, a committee chairman, a choir-master or a youth leader.

Always endeavour to have established policy at your fingertips and be ready to outline it clearly every time a new venture or development is discussed. Where others see only problems and difficulties aim to present strategies and solutions. You must be the one who sets the tone, the agenda and the targets of the team. Your task is to set legitimate and attainable expectations, ensuring that whatever it takes you do not lose sight of them.

Never meet for discussion with colleagues without giving thought beforehand as to what you want to be achieved by the conversation and the ultimate goal of your work together. Try to keep a balance between allowing adequate time for discussion and debate, and the need to make timely decisions.

Know when a task should be done

The cultivation of a sense of timing is invaluable. 'There is a time for everything, and a season for every activity under heaven … a time to tear down and a time to build' (Ecclesiastes 3:1, 3). It is not enough to know *what* needs to be done; *when* it is to be done is just as important. Inexperienced leaders sometimes rush into a project expecting to accomplish their vision at once without considering how reasonable it is to suppose that people will share the vision so quickly. The likely result will be that they grind to a slow halt and find that they have antagonized those who, given more time and patient and tactful handling, would have accomplished the task gladly.

Whatever your goal, ask yourself how you may reasonably expect things to develop. Introducing a new idea too early may do harm. In Christian service the bulldozer technique is always out of place. Sow the seed of your ideas early and do not urge their implementation upon people before they are ready to receive them. At the right time someone may well produce those ideas as his or her own and will be willing to achieve your vision with enthusiasm as if the vision were originally theirs. Never be in a hurry if you are not sure you have the support of others in what you propose. In my early years as a pastor, I represented British churches in a conference of churches in Germany. A German family gave me warm hospitality. One day the father of the family took me for a walk and I must have shared with him my hopes and aspirations for my church situation and probably some of my frustrations. I remember him stopping, turning to me, and quietly and gently saying something I have never forgotten, 'God is never in a hurry.'

Know how the task should be done

You need to know *what* needs to be done, *when* it should be done, and *how* to do it. To enthuse people about a task without being clear as to how they will accomplish it often results in a discouraging anticlimax. It is sometimes easier to stir people's enthusiasm than it is to know the way in which a job should be achieved. Before endeavouring to provoke people's interest in a project or venture, therefore, make sure you are as clear as it is possible to be, at that stage, of the way in which it can be accomplished. People will be sure to ask questions and if you are unable to answer, the enthusiasm you have generated will vanish as quickly as it arose and will be twice as hard to recreate.

Cultivate the ability to get a group of people working together towards a common objective with the full and maximum cooperation of each member of the group. Without knowledge of method, of how the goal is to be achieved, you have lost before you start.

These five factors in the basic practice of leadership bring to light eight practical consequences.

Know your own mind

There is a world of difference between going to a committee meeting with your mind made up and knowing your own mind. It is doubtful if you should ever go to a meeting with your mind finally made up for that presupposes that you will reject whatever else others may suggest. Knowing your own mind means being clear as to your present convictions so that you may contribute them coherently to a discussion, being willing at the same time to adjust your opinions and alter your convictions as new light is shed upon the subject through other people's contributions. If you are often in a state of indecision, you will lose people's confidence. Be clear as to your own views sufficiently well to change them where necessary for the good of the purpose to be achieved.

Show how things are to be done

While you should not do everything yourself, and so give the impression that no one else can do the job properly, you should on the other hand be able to demonstrate the way in which a task is to be done. Rather than simply telling people to do something, give them, where possible, a practical example.

Let us imagine that you are delegating secretarial work. If the person to whom you are entrusting the responsibility has little experience, you will be helping him or her very much if you explain something of your own method of handling correspondence — perhaps providing copies of standard letters you have written; not that you expect him or her to do things precisely as you do them but rather to offer a guide.

To show how things are to be done you should be an example and you should be prepared to give time and detailed instruction to people. As they take up tasks for the first time, they will appreciate guidance as to the best way of going about their work. Good leaders do not say, 'Go this way' but rather 'Follow me' (Mark 1:17-18; John 13:12-17). They should be those who say 'Come' rather than 'Go'. We get the best out of people when we give the best ourselves.

In showing how things are to be done, beware of demanding too much. While you should be demanding of yourself and impatient with your own mistakes, you should not be over-critical of others but patient, for only then will you obtain the best from them.

Be concerned for reasonable progress

You above everyone else should know how things are going: whether progress is being made, and — if it is reasonable progress — the way in which it is to be maintained. Those who work under your direction will be concerned for their personal spheres of responsibility; your duty is to see that each unit is working effectively to produce the progress that is to be expected of the whole.

When people feel that their leader is concerned for progress and is aware of the importance of their contribution they receive an excellent boost to their morale. All of us want to feel that we are achieving something worthwhile; we are glad when we have reason to believe that we are doing better now than we did in the past. Your objective should be to ensure that those led by you have grounds for this kind of encouragement. Be quick to show appreciation and to recognize successes, no matter how small.

It is up to you to see that every activity is forward-looking. In determining the path of progress, do not be put off by anticipated problems. They are the price of progress. Faith equates them with success. Be careful not to become so caught up with attention to detail and small matters that you fail to have time to consider the overall effectiveness of the work you lead. It may be necessary at times to withdraw from your sphere of activity so that you may look at it from a distance. If you feel you are too busy to do this, then you *are* too busy and will not see the work go forward.

The desire you have for progress, however, needs to be reasonable. While it is good for people to put in extra effort in a particular endeavour sometimes, they cannot remain under perpetual strain without exhaustion, with the consequence that they eventually perform their tasks with lethargy until the next special effort. Consistent and reasonable progress within the bounds of normal achievement is the proper goal. It will help if you communicate to those who work with you that problems are always to be expected and are not necessarily a sign of failure. No attempt should be made on their part therefore to cover them up but rather to deal with them, and, if they find they cannot, to share them with you.

Have some 'go' about you

English ambassador Randolph reported to his superiors in London of John Knox, the Scottish Reformation leader, 'The voice of that one man is able in one hour to put more life in us than five hundred trumpets continually blustering in our ears.' While few will have the special ability of John Knox, it is essential that you should be marked by energy and drive. This reference to the power of the human voice is a reminder that you should not regard voice skills as unimportant. Always aim at speaking coherently, clearly and sufficiently loud so that everyone is able to hear you. The New Testament axiom is not to be neglected, 'If the trumpet does not sound a clear call, who will get ready for battle?' (1 Corinthians 14:8).

Although you should hold back your temper when provoked, you should learn to let yourself go when you have a vision to share and a work to initiate. If you lack enthusiasm, you cannot expect a spark of enthusiasm to be struck when you try to get people behind you. Beware however of a forced eagerness since it soon wears thin. You will do better not to present any project to others until your own zeal is aroused and you are genuinely convinced of its value. When you are sure about what needs to be done, give careful attention to presenting the matter effectively, and when you do, let people see how keen you are. Enthusiastic and honest leadership inspires willing service and co-operation. Little wonder that Deborah and Barak sang, 'When the princes in Israel take the lead, when the people willingly offer themselves — praise the LORD' (Judges 5:2).

Be a confirmed optimist

Pessimists seldom have much 'go' about them; you need to be characterized by an optimism that springs from good judgement and faith. Faith, the gift of God, is indispensable for the exercise of leadership. While you should not be unrealistic, you should not look always on the worse side of things. When difficulties are experienced, there will be plenty who will want to give in and abandon an enterprise; you need to stand out because of your confidence that the future will yet be bright since difficulties so often prove to be the stepping stones to success.

Seek to be far-sighted

In handling any situation, do not think only of what seems to be the present solution, but try to determine the answer that is going to be permanently effective.

Review the areas of your responsibility and see if you can anticipate difficulties that are likely to arise; then analyse their probable causes. You may well be able to take immediate action, which will remove the causes of the snags and troubles you anticipate. Endeavour to be pro-active rather than re-active. William Carey, the pioneer missionary to India, provides an excellent example. He presented one of the most powerful arguments for the World Mission of the Church in a document entitled *An Enquiry into the Obligation of Christians to use means for the Conversion of the Heathens*. 'His leadership ability was seen in the manner in which he effectively removed the five main excuses he felt would be raised against missionary work: the distance of the "heathen" lands; their barbarous ways; the physical danger to missionaries; the difficulties of procuring necessary supplies; the barrier to communication of foreign language.'[3] His realistic assessment and anticipation of people's response meant that he had answers to give to those who were hesitant. He succeeded!

Have an eye on the future when you fix policy for the present. The quick policy decision, made without thought as to future repercussions, may lead to complications. The tower of the Brampton Church in Cumbria, England, was built under the direction of the architect Philip Webb, the pre-Raphaelite. His working drawings were a marvel of detail, showing even the six-inch nails in the carpentry. As a young man John Laing, the builder, expressed his admiration to Webb's chief assistant who simply answered: 'We are not considering only the first thousand years.'[4] In actions and decisions, do not consider only the present, but also the distant future.

Practise honesty with integrity

Openness and honesty are always the right and best policy. They have unique power to build up confidence. Inevitably, bad, sad and unhelpful events take place and the natural human tendency is either to play them down or hide the truth. Instead the questions should be asked, 'What is the truth about this situation?' and 'What ought to be made known straightaway?' With these questions answered, ask 'How much needs to be shared with others?' and 'When should it be done and in what context?' Although the implementation of right action may be difficult and costly it means that people know that they can trust their leadership.

Aim to encourage new leadership

An excellent definition of leadership is that it is the ability to encourage and equip other leaders. Paul implies that principle in his instruction to Timothy to which we have already referred, 'The things you have heard me say in the presence of many witnesses entrust to reliable men who will also be qualified to teach others' (2 Timothy 2:2). It is sadly possible to be in leadership and to enjoy being indispensable as everything revolves around you and everyone foolishly imagines that you alone can do what is necessary. The tragedy then is that when the time comes for you to be removed from the scene — and your mortality ensures that will be the case — much, if not all, of what you have built up and achieved will be lost. If, however, you are continually producing new leaders, the work that you do has a secret of successful continuance built into it.

It may prove to be a helpful exercise even now to write down the names of individuals in whom you see leadership potential, perhaps because of the evidence of certain spiritual gifts, good judgement, a capacity to anticipate problems and deal with them, and the drive to get things done. Having done that, ask yourself the question, 'What can I do to encourage them?'

Christ's example

We have only to consider our Lord Jesus Christ's leadership example to see how perfectly he put these principles into practice. He knew precisely what was expected of him. He understood what could be expected of people in general and especially of his disciples (John 2:24-25; Luke 22:32). He appreciated what his special task and responsibility was (Luke 9:51). He was aware of when his task had to be done (John 13:1) and how it should be done (Matthew 16:21). He knew his own mind (John 6:6). He showed how things were to be done (John 13:12-17). He was concerned for reasonable progress (Mark 1:38-39; 6:30-31). He always looked forward with hope, inspiring confidence (John 16:33; Luke 12:32). He practised honesty about the enterprise to which he called his disciples to be his fellow-workers (John 15:18; 16:33). He deliberately nurtured and equipped them for leadership (Mark 6:7, 30-31).

The practice of this kind of leadership will not fail to inspire confidence. Nothing influences people's confidence in their leaders more than their character. The more they inspire trust the more effective they will be.

Prayer

Lord Jesus, you taught your disciples the practice of leadership by your teaching and your example. Help me to fix my eyes upon you every day, the Author and perfector of our faith. As I strive to serve others in your name help me to test all my actions by your teaching and example. For your name's sake. Amen.

Questions for Bible study groups

Read Ecclesiastes 3:1-8; John 13:15; Romans 15:7; Philippians 2:1-11; Ephesians 4:32; 5:2, 25

1. *Ecclesiastes 3:1-8:* This passage lists a number of important issues when timing is important. Which of them is especially relevant to those who have the responsibility of leadership?
2. *John 13:15; Romans 15:7; Philippians 2:1-11; Ephesians 4:32; 5:2, 25* all refer in some way to the example of our Lord Jesus Christ. In what ways is he our example as Christian believers? Of which particular things do Christian leaders need to take note?
3. 'Leadership is the ability to encourage and equip other leaders.' How good a definition is this?

Questions for church leaders

1. *What does our membership rightly expect of us?*

2. *How do we define our priority tasks?*
3. *What practical steps can we take to further our knowledge of the people we serve?*
4. *What would we regard as reasonable progress for our work in this coming year?*
5. *How open and honest are we with one another and our membership?*

7.
Good personal relationships

Many principles of leadership deserve attention but in the next three chapters we select three essentials, beginning with good personal relationships.

Leaders as shepherds

Christian leaders are exhorted to 'be shepherds of God's flock that is under your care' (1 Peter 5:1-4; John 21:15-17). The relationship between shepherds and their flocks is close. Shepherds are well acquainted with the characteristics of their sheep; the sheep have a legitimate feeling of security when their shepherds are alongside them because they have practical experience of their care and concern. In the East, rather than the shepherd driving the sheep, the sheep follow the shepherd. This picture of the eastern shepherd, taken up in the Bible to depict the Christian leader, emphasizes the importance of happy personal relationships inspired by confidence and mutual trust. Without harmonious relationships, a leader's task is hopeless; furthermore, bad relationships bring dishonour to God's name. Bad personal relationships probably disqualify more people from leadership than any other reason.

In describing himself as the Good Shepherd, the Lord Jesus says that he knows his sheep and calls them by name (John 10:3, 14). For many of us it takes great effort to know and remember people's names but it is an invaluable asset and makes for good relationships. It is achievable especially if you link it with praying for individuals by name. When you meet people for the first time ask if they mind you writing down their names. On arriving back home, transfer their names into your prayer diary, perhaps adding a phrase or note to help you remember them. It is equally important to learn the names of children.

Remoteness is no recommendation of a person's leadership. In secular society leaders are often inaccessible and appear distant. However, leaders who inspire the greatest confidence are those who get out among people, look them in the eyes, listen to them and understand what their needs and problems are.

If your leadership involves responsibility for work delegated to others, part of your shepherding care is to keep in touch with those who lead it and, where possible, to make occasional visits to their sphere of responsibility. This should not be done so infrequently that they immediately imagine that a visit means that you suspect that there is something wrong with their work. Rather, your visits should assure them of your deep interest in what they do.

Importance of Christian character

Good personal relationships arise from a person's character. Those who live up to the prescribed standards for leaders continually cultivate good relationships.

Hospitality, because it provides opportunities for getting to know people at an informal level, always helps. The Bible urges us to 'practise hospitality' (Romans 12:13; see also 1 Timothy 3:2; Titus 1:8; 1 Peter 4:9; Hebrews 13:2). The deliberate endeavour to recognize and love the good in people (Titus 1:8) and to encourage them in the faith (Acts 20:31) brings out the best in them. When you have yourself under control so that you are not soon angry (Titus 1:7), nor too quick to show your feelings (Titus 1:8; 1 Timothy 3:2), nor impatient (1 Timothy 3:3; Titus 3:2), you build up harmonious relationships through every contact you make.

If you pause a moment you will be able to list habits, actions and attitudes that have marred your human relationships in the past. You will save yourself from many mistakes if you identify them as dangers and treat them accordingly. You may be able to add several harmful items to the list we now make.

A domineering spirit

Avoid at all costs being overbearing and tyrannical. The problem is that if you are domineering you probably do not intend to be and do not realize that you are! So, if you think this delusion does not apply to you, be prepared to think again! As a person of action and enthusiasm, you may be quickly impatient at any restraint placed upon you by others and critical of any suggestion that might hinder the full implementation of your ideas. People ought not to be afraid to express their opinions through fear of what your reaction will be or of what attitude you will adopt towards them. If they do not express their opinions in front of you because of your domineering spirit, they will be sure to do so in your absence, worsening your relationship. Examine yourself to ensure you do not want your own way all the time. Peter tells us that there is no place in Christian leadership for 'lording' it over people (1 Peter 5:3).

Stubbornness

Leadership should not be synonymous with self-assertion. You will never be immune from making mistakes whether in actions or judgement. Bad relationships are created through the refusal of leaders to acknowledge their faults, either through pride or a misguided idea that to admit a mistake undermines people's confidence. To hang on stubbornly to a course of action or a manner of doing things when the decision to do so was clearly wrong creates long-lasting friction. When you have made up your mind on a subject, do not resist those who put forward ideas that they consider improvements. You must be open to reason and show yourself to be so. Clearly, you cannot implement every suggestion made to you, but take notice of what colleagues say and be honest in your consideration of each idea. You should not have a reputation for being overbearing or stubborn (Titus 1:7).

Criticism

You need to be capable of constructive criticism more than most. Nevertheless, ruthlessly resist the temptation to engage in criticism of an absent colleague, unless it is in the privacy and confidence of a meeting with other leaders because you are concerned to help the person in question.

A subtle form of criticism — not always recognized as such but extremely damaging — is the making of comparisons. If you exercised leadership in another place or sphere, you will seldom help matters by regularly referring to it and declaring how excellent were the people who worked with you. By all means learn from your past experience but do not compare one with another.

Sometimes people will come to you with a criticism or a grievance against a colleague, wanting your agreement with what they say. Make a point of never agreeing immediately and, at the same time, endeavour to say something positive and favourable about the person criticized. Say also, where it is right to do so, that you will look into the matter and have a word with your colleague. If you do not do this and readily agree with the criticism, your agreement will be rapidly broadcast and will probably reach the ears of the person criticized. Not only will it then be difficult to help that person, but even the criticizers may lose confidence in you for listening to them!

On those occasions when criticism is voiced about those who share leadership with you and for whom you have responsibility, the best thing you can do is to take the blame yourself. This is beneficial in at least two ways. First, the people who make the criticism may express it to you because they are unwilling or afraid to make it to the individuals concerned. That at least means that they have got it out of their system and it can be dealt with, where necessary. Second, the people who perhaps deserve the criticism recognize your loyalty to them and your relationship of trust with them is strengthened.

Double-talk

It is not always easy to be frank and honest, but this does not excuse us from trying. To say one thing to people's face and another behind their back is ruinous for harmonious relationships. Probably, however, this form of double-talk may not be your problem; more likely, you will be inclined to water down the truth to people's face, and give the whole of the truth in their absence. A direct question demands a direct answer on most occasions. It is downright cowardice to shrink from speaking honestly to someone; and it is double-talk to say to others what you have refrained from saying to the person concerned. Although honest speaking may be difficult and not at first appreciated, a right-thinking person ultimately appreciates it, and the best of relationships results.

Tactlessness

When you discover that you have irritated people, it is no excuse to say, 'Well, as Christians they have no right to feel like that. Why should I be bothered?' Although you should be firm and strict with your own weaknesses, you need to be patient with the weaknesses of others. Always speak the truth, as we have said; but that does not mean saying *everything* that there is to say, especially if some of the things may be unnecessarily hurtful. Moreover, in being honest, the response of your hearer depends on the manner in which you present the facts. If you find yourself enjoying putting people right, stop immediately and go no further until you can approach them with humility and with a genuine desire to see them helped and encouraged (Galatians 6:1).

Tactlessness comes about usually through speaking without thought. Try to put yourself in other people's place and think carefully before you make a judgement or express an opinion. The authority you have as a leader is not to put down but to build up.

Nowhere perhaps is tact more important than in implementing change. Change is inevitable for as Heraclitus, a Greek philosopher (540-480 BC), declared, 'Everything is in flux — you cannot step into the same river twice.'[1] The proverb 'A new broom sweeps clean' reminds us that it is when we are first in a new position of leadership that we may be tempted to make radical changes. Many sad and divisive situations will be avoided if you steel yourself to refrain from early changes before you really understand and appreciate the truth about your new situation.

Situations cannot be changed for the better unless we understand the realities behind them. One of the immediate reasons for your wanting to change something is that you have known or been used to something different and perhaps superior elsewhere. But the Holy Spirit who guided you where you were then may equally well have guided the people with whom you are now. Furthermore, more important than ways of doing things are good relationships between those who work together. If you succeed in implementing change and at the same time spoil relationships, the changes will achieve little.

This is not to suggest that change is not necessary but it does not have to happen all at once. It is also not to imply that resistance to change is commendable because it is not. Most, if not all, resist change, and those who deny it probably most! But ideally a prelude to change should be the gaining of people's confidence so that they do not have reason to doubt the motives behind the proposals. You need to balance two complementary truths: if something is not right, then endeavour to change it; if, however, something does not need to be changed, do not change it. You are not in a position to implement these truths without gaining a lot of information, listening to what people have to say, and engaging in open consultation.

Impartiality

Paul gave to Timothy the precise instruction that he was not to pre-judge issues that arose and that he was to act with strict impartiality (1 Timothy 5:21). Be impartial not only in fact, but also aim at giving the impression of impartiality.

Impartiality becomes easier if you try to recognize your natural prejudices so that you control them when they are likely to surface. You may, for example, have a natural prejudice against a method of going about a task. If you retain that prejudice and fail to have an open mind on the matter, you are unlikely to be unbiased when you have to deal with someone who does the job in the way you disapprove.

When going to a meeting at which an issue has to be decided, do not allow individuals to talk to you beforehand, wanting to give you their point of view in order to persuade you to be on their side. Stress that whatever they want to say ought to be said at the meeting in the presence of everyone. If people gain the impression that you give an ear to anyone who tries to impress you in private, they will not believe you to be impartial.

Once you make a practice of impartiality — no matter how ruthless you may have to be and how much it upsets at first even those who most keenly support you — you will find that you gain everyone's confidence. None will resent straightforward honesty that hurts if they know that you treat everyone in the same way.

Alertness to needs

Be tireless in your concern for those whom you lead (Hebrews 13:17); where there is evidence of a genuine concern for people's well-being good relationships result. Our Lord's concern for the individual meant that all who experienced it rejoiced in the relationship they had with him.

The more sympathy and thoughtfulness you show, the more harmonious will be your relationships. Patience and encouragement draw out the best from people. When it is necessary to criticize, it is equally important to build individuals up first with the praise they deserve. Hudson Taylor, the pioneer missionary leader, 'evoked almost blind loyalty because there was "none so sympathetic, none so tenderly affectionate, as he, concerning our wants and our work"'; thus wrote one of his workers.[2] Take trouble and time to appreciate the circumstances and feelings of those for whom you have responsibility.

Speed of apology

You will make mistakes; you will need to admit therefore that you have been wrong. As soon as you discover your error, make speedy amends, either by rectifying the situation in a practical manner or by making an apology.

It is a false sense of importance that makes leaders feel it beneath them to apologize. That appears to have been a conspicuous fault of Charles Stewart Parnell, the nineteenth-century Irish politician, called 'the uncrowned King of Ireland'. On one memorable occasion, he owed those who worked with him an apology for an unexplained absence. 'As soon as he arrived he retired to his room, offering no word of explanation or excuse to his colleagues. It had not taken many years for a modest, self-depreciating young man to develop the tactics of a dictator.' When he was urged to send a message explaining his delay, his response was, 'Never explain, never apologise. I could never keep my rabble together if I were not above the human weakness of an apology.'[3] That is the attitude of a dictator rather than a leader.

Failure to apologize may ruin harmony and goodwill, whereas a speedy and sincere apology may do much to cement a relationship and to re-establish it upon a firmer footing than before. Furthermore, if you are quick to see your faults, you will be encouraging those whom you lead to do likewise, and all will benefit as increasing harmony is fostered.

Avoidance of controversy

At all costs, avoid quarrels (1 Timothy 3:3; Titus 3:2). Even if you win the quarrel and 'get one over' your opponents, you will lose goodwill and your 'victory' will be of dubious value.

Learn to recognize those who tend to be quarrelsome and go out of your way to agree with them where that is possible with integrity. Endeavour to win their confidence by sharing with them as much as you can. If people become heated over a subject, try to postpone further discussion, if possible, suggesting that everyone goes away to think and pray about it. If you know that discussion of a subject is going to cause trouble with particular individuals try to arrange to discuss the issue with them with someone else present — preferably a colleague in leadership — so that the problem does not become a personal issue between you and the disgruntled people. If you feel yourself getting worked up, stop at once, until you have cooled down.

Unfortunately, controversy cannot always be avoided. Paul shunned quarrels but he sometimes found himself compelled to engage in dispute. There were occasions when he had to defend his God-given convictions, as, for example, when he withstood Peter to his face (Galatians 2:11). You should never want or look for an argument or a controversy; but there may be times when you have to state your convictions even though to do so means open disagreement with others. In such circumstances, you should be careful to speak the truth in love (Ephesians 4:15), and to harbour no malice against those who oppose you (Matthew 5:44; 1 Peter 2:20; 3:9).

Consistency

The relationship between Paul and the Corinthians was a close one — that of a spiritual parent and his children — but some fractious members of the Corinthian church sought to spoil it. Nevertheless, Paul's position was immeasurably strengthened because of the proof he could give of his consistency of speech and behaviour (2 Corinthians 1:17-20).

As a leader, you are a marked individual; inevitably, you are somewhat conspicuous. People tend to watch you more than they watch others; they automatically expect more of you than they do of themselves. They compare the manner that you deal with them on one occasion with that of a previous occasion. If there is any contradiction, they lose confidence in you.

Watch carefully your speech and behaviour. The words you use are enormously important. While you might argue that among friends you should not need to be careful about what you say, words once spoken cannot easily be retracted. Your words are not only capable of inspiring trust, they are critically important when you need to convey your vision and convictions about the way forward. Say what you mean, and mean what you say.

Be clear as to your opinions, but do not become too resolute about something before you have thought it through. Beware of fluctuations in your views. Try to deal with similar situations in the same way. Consistency inspires confidence.

Inconsistency will usually arise when you have not really thought out your attitudes and when you act on impulse influenced by the desire to comply with other people's wishes. Think through policy, and act as in the sight of God; then inconsistency will be removed.

A sense of humour

The ability to see a joke and to laugh at yourself is indispensable. While important in all relationships, it is especially valuable in leadership. A sense of humour relieves many a tense situation. When people perceive that you are ready to laugh at yourself, they will be much kinder in their criticism. If you do not cultivate a controlled sense of humour, you will tend to take yourself too seriously, and in leadership that may make you seem aloof and remote.

Some of us have to keep a tight rein on our sense of humour, while others have to encourage it. Whichever way it is, the effort is worthwhile, for a gentle sense of humour will deliver you from making mountains out of molehills and will provide a sense of perspective when you are in danger of exaggerating difficulties and problems.

Communicativeness

Communication skills can be learned and acquired. Think of people whom you know to be good at getting things across. Then ask yourself, 'What makes them so helpful and informative?'

Learn to organize your thoughts and to understand your audience so that you present the pros and cons of a course of action in a way that all can understand. Do not despise small or seemingly minor opportunities to communicate publicly since effective communication to hundreds is little different from communication to two or three people. The principles are much the same.

If ever you feel that you are not communicating well with your fellow leaders and perhaps with just one in particular, do not brush under the carpet the friction you see developing. Confront the problem by arranging to meet with the person or persons concerned and express your regret and your desire to be communicating well together.

Wherever possible bring those whom you lead into your confidence about the affairs for which you are responsible. Tell everyone who works under you as much as possible of the plans you have, and the relationship of their contribution to the goal behind the plans. Do not keep everything to yourself.

Let people know all that they can be told. Never give information that it is indiscreet to give, especially when it relates to individuals; but give all the information it is right and possible to provide. Such communicativeness creates harmony. Strong, silent types do not usually make good leaders. Where it is appropriate, tell people a little more than they might expect you to tell them, and you will win their trust, since you show confidence in them. As soon as the disciples realized the identity of their Master, he told them all that was going to happen to him; and he continued to do so (Matthew 16:21).

Not only should people be told all that they can be told but as soon as possible. If truth is withheld or delayed, others may announce it, and you will be considered to have concealed it.

Avoid resorting to spin when the truth is not very palatable or may indicate mistakes and fault on your part.

Often there is a need to communicate initially to people in small groups. Obviously there is a place for sharing important news, hopes and ideas with your complete constituency where possible. At the same time if there are smaller groups that meet regularly together or can be readily convened, they will appreciate the closer contact with the leader or leaders and the opportunity to ask questions and express views in a way they would not feel able to do in a larger group.

Imagine your church has a home for senior citizens and changes are imminent. It is not sufficient to share these changes in a church meeting without also, and preferably earlier, doing so with the residents of the home. If changes in direction or approach are required in the young people's work, it is not enough to announce this at a meeting of the whole church without also calling together the young people and explaining the changes to them.

We referred earlier to the difficulties of change. An essential key to achieving it is thoughtful communication beforehand. Write down the names of all who may be in any way affected by the proposed changes and before taking any action to achieve the changes, arrange to see each individual and communicate your motives and intentions. Give personal time to everyone who may feel threatened through what is planned.

The essence of communication is simplicity. Never forget that what seems simple and straightforward to you after perhaps weeks and months of thinking, arguing and agonizing may not appear simple to others when you present to them your final ideas. Good leaders can take something complicated and explain it so that their hearers understand. Michael Korda, author and editor-in-chief of Simon and Schuster, a large publishing house, wrote a perceptive definition: 'Great leaders are almost always great simplifiers, who cut through argument, debate and doubt, to offer a solution everybody can understand.'[4]

Readiness to say 'Thank you'

The value we place upon people is reflected in the appreciation we show of them. Everyone likes to be appreciated; and few people produce their best without the encouragement of someone's approval and thanks. Be quick to give people credit for what they do. A quick phone call, an e-mail, or brief note of thanks probably mean more than you imagine. Your aim should be to get people to want to go along with you, rather than to force them. Besides being the right thing, the readiness to express thanks does much to make people want to co-operate.

Anticipate the best

Generally speaking, you get what you expect from people. If you let people know that you anticipate their achieving what they know to be their best, you have done much to encourage them. They will be grateful to you, probably without realizing it, for providing them with the incentive they needed. They will enjoy working with you because you bring out the best in them.

Avoid being prejudiced too much by people's past failures. Naturally you cannot completely ignore mistakes and occasions when you have been let down; nevertheless, where possible, give the benefit of the doubt and you will get some surprises, as well as grateful and loyal supporters.

Patience

Getting the best from those working with you requires much patience and is an aspect of Christian love (1 Corinthians 13:4). The golden rule of good personal relationships is 'Do to others what you would have them do to you'; and automatically this gives priority to patience, which has been described aptly as waiting when you are in a hurry. It is being *long*-tempered rather than *short*-tempered. 'A man of knowledge uses words with restraint, and a man of understanding is even-tempered' (Proverbs 17:27).

Patience is needed in the face of inefficiency. 'In late middle age Hudson Taylor once confessed that "My greatest temptation is to lose my temper over the slackness and inefficiency so disappointing in those on whom I depended. It is no use to lose my temper — only kindness — but O, it is such a trial."'[5]

Much of what we have expressed may be summed up in the fact that a leader's personal relationships are to be governed by a devout and godly sincerity, by the grace of God, and not by worldly wisdom (2 Corinthians 1:12). You are never to scheme at playing off one person against another in order to come out on top; rather you are to think and act as in the sight of God, knowing that from such sincerity will issue relationships that display the unity of the Spirit. Towards the end of his life Dr Sangster, a Methodist preacher and leader, wrote, 'It has been coming ever clearer to me that what we are is so infinitely more important than what we do: that what we do at its best is only a reflex of what we are.'[6]

Where the best of relationships exist between leaders and those they lead, tensions that arise between workers may be readily resolved. The tension over the issue of status that existed between James and John on one hand and the rest of the disciples on the other, our Lord Jesus Christ could resolve because of the ideal relationship he had with them all (Mark 10:35-45).

Prayer

Heavenly Father, who gave your Son, Jesus Christ, to be the Saviour, Leader and Shepherd of his people, help me to follow in his footsteps in any leadership responsibilities you give to me. Make me sensitive to faults like stubbornness, favouritism and double-talk. Help me to be quick to apologize when I make mistakes, to expect the best from others with patience and to be quick to say 'Thank you'. I ask this in my Saviour's name and for his sake, Amen.

Questions for Bible study groups

Read John 10:1-18; 21:15-17; 1 Peter 5:1-4

1. *John 10:1-18*: In what ways is the Lord Jesus Christ the model Shepherd? What especially inspires our confidence in him?
2. *John 21:15-17*: What is the priority of shepherds of Christ's flock? How do you expect them to exercise this responsibility?
3. *1 Peter 5:1-4*: What are the characteristics of shepherds of Christ's flock? How should these affect your attitude to your church leadership?

4. What in your experience tends most to spoil personal relationships? What positive remedies can you suggest?

Questions for church leaders

1. *How can we ensure that the shepherding of God's people — their pastoral care — is our top priority?*
2. *How important are our relationships as leaders for those we lead?*
3. *How well and wisely do we introduce change?*

8.
Delegation

'Oh, well, they have done it for years; they will never hand it over now.' Sadly, that has often been said of established leaders. Doggedness in hanging on to a task may arise from genuine faithfulness. However, it is not commendable in those called to leadership. Leadership involves taking initiative in recognizing and setting apart the right people for specific service. As in the case of Elijah and Elisha, one of the duties God sometimes places upon us is the duty of seeing our successor raised up (1 Kings 19:19). William Booth, founder of the Salvation Army, gave good advice to George Scott Railton when he assumed responsibility for the Army's work in America, 'Never forget that it is not what you do yourself as much as what you get others to do that will be the making of the Army.'[1]

Most of us tend to be slow in delegating responsibility. Jethro, Moses' father-in-law, visited Moses and his family and found him doing the work of a judge over the people of Israel *from morning to night*. Exodus 18 tells the story.

'The next day Moses took his seat to serve as judge for the people, and they stood round him from morning till evening. When his father-in-law saw all that Moses was doing for the people, he said, "What is this you are doing for the people?

Why do you alone sit as judge, while all these people stand round you from morning till evening?"

'Moses answered him, "Because the people come to me to seek God's will. Whenever they have a dispute, it is brought to me, and I decide between the parties and inform them of God's decrees and laws."

'Moses' father-in-law replied, "What you are doing is not good. You and these people who come to you will only wear yourselves out. The work is too heavy for you; you cannot handle it alone. Listen now to me and I will give you some advice, and may God be with you. You must be the people's representative before God and bring their disputes to him. Teach them the decrees and laws, and show them the way to live and the duties they are to perform. But select capable men from all the people — men who fear God, trustworthy men who hate dishonest gain — and appoint them as officials over thousands, hundreds, fifties and tens. Have them serve as judges for the people at all times, but have them bring every difficult case to you; the simple cases they can decide themselves. That will make your load lighter, because they will share it with you. If you do this and God so commands, you will be able to stand the strain, and all these people will go home satisfied."

'Moses listened to his father-in-law and did everything he said. He chose capable men from all Israel and made them leaders of the people, officials over thousands, hundreds, fifties and tens. They served as judges for the people at all times. The difficult cases they brought to Moses, but the simple ones they decided themselves' (Exodus 18:13-26).

Moses was sensible enough to listen and put into practice the advice he received. He had to develop, as do all leaders, the ability to choose people to whom he could wisely delegate some of his responsibilities. One of the conclusions of an influential report commissioned by the Church of Scotland on its corporate life was that 'ministers must learn to devolve more tasks to their elders and to unleash the creative potential that is surely there in most congregations, dormant and untapped'.[2]

Slowness to delegate

Leaders sometimes have surprising difficulty in delegation. Dawson Trotman was the dynamic founder of The Navigators, who taught, 'Never do anything someone else can do or will do when there is so much others cannot or will not do.' Yet, perhaps without realizing the inconsistency, he 'insisted on making all decisions personally, down to the colour of paint for storage shelves and the choice of paper and ink for every printing job'.[3] Unless you learn to delegate responsibility, you will fail to be an efficient leader. Reasons for reluctance to delegate are not difficult to recognize. You may lack confidence in others, or may feel that no one has the ability to do the job as you do it. This attitude is quite wrong since it implies that you believe you are indispensable — and you are not. If you encourage people to depend upon you too much you will become a peg upon which too much hangs, so that when the peg gives way everything collapses (Isaiah 22:23-25).

You may, on the other hand, find such pleasure in a task that you are reluctant to give it up. You may even dislike the thought of someone else taking it over, and perhaps doing it differently. The reasons behind slowness to delegate, therefore, may be possessiveness and the fear of being displaced, both of which are unworthy feelings.

Your attitude may be expressed then in the words, 'If you want something done well, do it yourself.' However, this is not an acceptable principle of leadership for, firstly, it is a form of pride, and secondly, if that is your attitude, people will let you do the work and will never rise to it themselves.

Evils of no delegation

Without delegation, everything grinds slowly and sometimes almost imperceptibly to a standstill. Progress is not made, and at best your work is maintained for the present but the seeds of its disintegration are sown. You will end up concentrating only on keeping things going and will have no real vision for the future. Jobs will not be done efficiently because no one person has sufficient energy to do so much. If you do not delegate you will not have time to review development and progress. You will get into the habit of having to deal always with the immediate, so that more important tasks will be pushed out because they are not marked 'Urgent'.

The criminal aspect of the failure to delegate is that the potential others have is left undeveloped. God, who has given you ability, has given it to others too; it is your responsibility to recognize their potential and to see that it is developed and given scope. You especially need to give time to fostering and nurturing the gifts of younger people. This has particular rewards, not least in the freshness they will renew in you as you remember your own early ventures into leadership.

Leadership and delegation

John Stott, Rector Emeritus of All Souls' Church, Langham Place, London, UK, had a succession of curates who testified to the speed at which he would aim to pass on responsibility to them. Significantly his biographer writes, 'Since his days as head of school at Rugby, and again as camp secretary, John Stott had been concerned to master the art of delegation. One reason why so much was committed to paper in terms of briefings, instructions and memoranda, was to make it possible for his curates to learn and become responsible for the different aspects of All Souls' ministry, and to set such boundaries to their freedom of action as would ensure a proper continuity.'[4]

Recognize the importance of delegation. John Mott wrote, 'It is better to set ten men to work than to do the work of ten men even if one is able to do so.'[5] Do not do a job yourself, more or less automatically, simply because others fail to co-operate; before resorting to such an expedient try your hardest to get others to assist.

Leaders are 'overseers' (1 Timothy 3:1); their responsibility is to superintend rather than to do everything themselves. Not to have any idea about how to go about delegation is a serious leadership disqualification. As Barnabas had his eye on Paul from the start, recognizing his potential, we should be on the lookout for those who may carry responsibility.

Examples

In every sphere of life a chain of command exists. Prime or first ministers delegate to their Cabinet; their Cabinet members delegate to undersecretaries and assistants. The principle of delegation proceeds right down to the newest entrant to the civil service. We referred earlier to Moses' attention to the advice of his father-in-law (Exodus 18:13-26). Our Lord Jesus Christ spent three years thoroughly training the apostles so that they, in turn, would be able to delegate the responsibility of the preaching of the gospel to trustworthy people. Paul felt a continuing responsibility for the churches that he saw established through his missionary endeavours; but, at the earliest opportunity, he placed the direct responsibility for their care upon others. He did not hurry this delegation — it normally took place on his second visit — but he never delayed it longer than was necessary (Acts 14:23).

Principles of delegation

Delegation requires care. Paul's instruction not to be over-hasty in laying on hands in ordination is applicable to the assigning of responsibility in Christian service (1 Timothy 5:22).

Ample instruction

When delegating, give time to explaining in detail the assignment that is to be delegated. Basic to the call to leadership our Lord Jesus Christ gave to the Twelve was 'that they might be with him' before ever he sent them out to preach (Mark 3:14). He gave time to instructing them. It was one of his priorities. As a leader, you should be 'able to teach' (1 Timothy 3:2), and this aptness needs to include not only ability to teach the Word of God but also to teach a task that is being handed on. Besides being unfair, it can be rather frightening and discouraging to be delegated responsibility without guidance as to the manner in which it is to be carried out.

I look back gratefully to the time that I was a student and a member of a Christian Union. For a year I served as its secretary. What helped me most was the action of my predecessor in handing on to me a folder that contained a draft letter for writing to prospective speakers, with details of what was required of them, and a similar draft letter of thanks after they had made their visit. It not only showed me how to go about things but it saved me from neglecting obvious but important details. I also had the opportunity of working with others in a University Mission committee where one of my responsibilities was to make a scrapbook of all our publicity and other things we did to make the mission known so that those who did the same thing in three years' time had something to work on. This kind of attention to detail is invaluable and enormously helpful in delegation and handing on responsibility.

Make clear the smallest details. Show an awareness of the problems that may be experienced. Everyone needs to have standards at which to aim. Explain what, in your opinion, will constitute the task well done; set out high but attainable objectives. Although a lot of time has to be spent in the early stages of delegation, if done properly, the benefits will soon be seen, more than compensating for time initially spent in giving instruction.

An initial element of control

If the delegated task involves considerable responsibility, it is probably wise to maintain an element of discreet control at the beginning. It is sometimes possible to suggest a period of transition during which the task will be handed over and a final date when it is hoped that the new person may assume complete responsibility. At the same time it must be emphasized that a person should be given as free a hand as possible once a task has been assigned. This process underlines the importance of wise choice, careful proving and giving possible candidates for leadership earlier responsibilities in order to test their character and ability.

Regular review

In the course of a Pastoral Theology lecture in Durham University Dr John Stott said, 'I myself have only recently learned that the true art of delegation is not to hand over work to somebody else and then forget about it, but to commit work to a deputy who knows that he is responsible to you and can at times report back and seek advice.'[6] An essential part of delegation is checking that things are on the rails, that is to say, reassessing the delegated tasks, and, where necessary, bringing them back on to the rails before anything serious occurs.

There is value — providing it can be established at the beginning as a regular practice — in instituting a regular review of what has been delegated, so that progress and difficulties may be reported and problems anticipated before they become realities. If you do this, however, use great discretion. Be at pains to make it clear that the review does not spring from any lack of confidence but through interest and the desire to help. Be quick to commend progress, no matter how small, when a task has been handed over.

Calculated risks

At times you will have to be willing to take a calculated risk. A missionary organization has been conspicuous for its growth and one of the contributory factors is easy to perceive. Traditionally it has put heavy burdens on young directors. It has been precisely by such an approach that God has helped them to develop the leadership needed for a huge and growing task. In their view, an occasional failure of the system — or even serious errors of judgement of individual administrators — does not mean that this productive method should be abandoned. The risk must be taken, otherwise progress will be hindered. Failure to take the risks of delegation results in stagnation.

Firm support

Make sure you stand by the right decisions of those to whom you and others with you delegate responsibility. There will always be those who resist the new and try to hang on to the old; they may well try to criticize the decisions and actions of a newly appointed person. As a leader, you have a responsibility to resist all such approaches and to stand by those who have just taken up their duties. In reading *Leadership,* the autobiography of Rudolph Giuliani, the mayor of New York at the time of 9/11, I was struck by his simple statement, 'When I delegate, I delegate.'[7]

This firm support of those appointed and the determination not to interfere must not mean, however, that you fail to offer the support people may need. You must make sure that people understand exactly what is expected of them for they may sometimes be too shy and hesitant to ask and as a result suffer agonies of spirit through self-doubt.

Priority of delegation

Delegation is a 'must'. The church as a whole and many local churches are in desperate need of leaders. Wise delegation gives rise to leaders. Delegation ensures a succession. As soon as someone is carrying out delegated tasks satisfactorily, it is wise, if you have the personnel, to train up others to assist them so that they will have natural successors. Even if those assistants do not become their successor they will be equipped to fill other positions when the need arises.

Besides inspiring confidence in the leadership, delegation leaves leaders free to develop fresh avenues of service or activity. It is absolutely necessary if you are to be free to take fresh initiatives. Leadership should mean assuming new responsibilities and undertaking forward developments; but these are possible only when responsibility for established projects and tasks is placed elsewhere. Leaders should pioneer; then, once their pioneer work has become established, they should shed responsibility for the recently established work so that they may pioneer once again.

How things go when you are not present is perhaps the best indication of the wisdom and effectiveness of your delegation. Leadership may be defined as the ability to train others to lead and to develop everyone's highest potential; such a goal may be achieved only where delegation is deliberately practised. Sir John Marshall was an eminent archaeologist. The judgement of his peers was that he was unsuccessful in leadership because he failed to nurture people in his professional wake. Sir Mortimer Wheeler, influential in Indian archaeology, declared, 'It has been said of him, with some truth, that he was "a tree under which nothing grew".'[8] Determine to be a tree under which much may grow!

Prayer

Gracious Father, thank you for all those people who have encouraged me by their trust and delegation of responsibilities to me. Please help me to follow their example and to encourage others in the same way. Make me sensitive to their need for encouragement and may I know your help in maintaining the best possible relationship with them. For our Lord Jesus Christ's sake.

Questions for Bible study groups

Read Exodus 18:13-26; Acts 14:21-23

1. *Exodus 18:13-26*: What principles of delegation may we learn from Jethro's advice to Moses?
2. As you think of your church fellowship, in which areas does there need to be greater delegation or do you need to delegate responsibility?
3. *Acts 14:21-23*: Why do you think Paul and Barnabas did not appoint elders in each church on their first visit but did so on their second?
4. How do we know they treated this task with seriousness? What lessons should we learn from this?
5. Can you think of people who have especially helped you when you have been given new responsibility? How have they done so?

Questions for church leaders

1. *Are there tasks that we are hanging on to that we ought to have delegated?*
2. *In which areas would delegation be helpful and timely?*

3. *In what ways are we giving time and scope to younger people and the fostering of their gifts?*

4. *Where can we appoint assistants to people who carry heavy responsibilities so as to relieve them and to test the reliability and ability of others?*

9.
Efficiency

Paul's exhortation to the Corinthians that 'Everything should be done in a fitting and orderly way' (1 Corinthians 14:40) has special reference to the conduct of Christian worship but the principle has wider application.

Leadership is necessary for order (Titus 1:5), and your responsibility as a leader is to see that everything is done well and in a God-honouring fashion.

The word 'steward' is used to describe a Christian leader. The contemporary word would be 'manager' or 'administrator'. A steward is responsible for the efficient care of his employer's affairs. You likewise need to understand the principles governing your Master's work to be able to apply them faithfully and efficiently.

Efficiency is so important that Paul regarded it as a necessary qualification for leadership. He instructed Timothy that none were to be called to the office of a bishop (or elder) or deacon unless they were already demonstrating evidence of managing their own house and home well (1 Timothy 3:4, 12).

Four areas of efficiency

1. Be efficient in preparation

Even as the most important part of a building is its invisible foundation, so the most substantial contribution to your efficiency is your unseen preparation. Endeavours that seem to observers to be smooth and easy to accomplish usually have behind them much careful homework. This is true of public utterances and speeches. Those that appear the most effortless are usually the most carefully prepared and rehearsed. While others may forget to prepare, you should not. Sometimes you may delegate a task to others, but it is up to you to see that it is done and checked. Nothing should be left to chance.

2. Be efficient in carrying a task through to its end

Never leave a job uncompleted, unless it is essential to do so. Many possess enthusiasm and energy to start a task or to get others to do it, but fewer possess the staying power to see it through and to maintain the enthusiasm of others.

3. Be efficient in organization

Organize thoroughly: never be content with muddling through somehow or hoping that things will come together without careful thought. Planning is essential whether we build a house, put together a piece of flat-pack furniture or learn a foreign language. In organizing or conducting a meeting, plan as much of its detail as possible beforehand. Rather than being a waste of time, this will actually save time when the meeting takes place. Sitting on or chairing committees will often be part of your responsibility; prepare for them by considering the likely matters that will arise. Go to the meeting prepared to help other members by having positive suggestions in mind if no one else comes forward with something more constructive.

4. Be efficient in administration

Administration requires a light yet effective control of the activities of those working under your leadership. Many things requiring action will occur to you when you are not able to give attention to them. Few of us have good enough memories to carry such items in our minds until we have the time to deal with them. It is a good idea to make a note of anything you are likely to forget; in particular, write down everything you have promised to do.

Essential principles

Determine what must be done

In tackling any task, first determine precisely what has to be done. If you do not have a clear target before you, there is little likelihood of your hitting it. Rather than rush into action, take time to sit down and think a situation through. Once you have decided upon the appropriate objectives and methods, set yourself to their achievement.

Give attention to detail

Think of every possible hitch or scenario that ought to be catered for. Imagine, for the sake of illustration, that you are a youth leader and are planning a sports afternoon. Efficiency demands that you ask yourself what could mar the enjoyment of the afternoon, so that you may avoid such a catastrophe. An obvious question is, 'What will we do if it rains?' Not to have an answer — for example, an alternative programme — may not only cause confusion but it will destroy confidence in your leadership, because of your thoughtlessness.

Aim at simplicity of organization and administration

When deciding between various methods that may achieve what is necessary, choose the simplest. Be willing to abandon a complicated way of doing things — perhaps acquired haphazardly over a long period — for a more direct and simple method, perhaps suggested by a colleague.

Do not put off the difficult for the sake of the easy

Snags and difficulties never cease to present themselves. It is perilous to postpone action on a task that is difficult and time-consuming, making the excuse that you must deal with routine matters that are pressing but which do not require the mental effort of the really important business. Resist the temptation to put off demanding tasks. The longer the postponement the more ominous they become. Furthermore, you will be sowing seeds of stress because eventually you will have to deal with them through the pressure of a date deadline; the effort necessary at the last moment will exhaust you, and as a result, you will tax your overall efficiency. The difficult is never as difficult as it appears; once we apply ourselves to the problem, we usually find the solution unfolding itself.

Deal thoroughly with the task

To deal with a situation by half measures accentuates a problem and in the end takes much more time than to deal properly with it in the first place. Do not put down a task until you feel you have dealt with it adequately. Dr Codrington, a headmaster of St Barnabas School, Norfolk Island, was a great gardener. Dr Charles Fox, a master at the school, writes of how he later lived in Dr Codrington's old house. 'I had his house and garden and greenhouse and was as fond of flowers as he had been, and like him was much troubled by the snails which infested the flower garden. I asked a lad who had been his gardener how he had dealt with them. Joe said the Doctor used to give the boys sixpence to collect a bucket of snails and bring them to him. "And then how did you destroy them?" I asked. "We didn't," said Joe. "We always put them back in the garden for the other boys."'[1] Effective as the Doctor's scheme to remove the snails was, it failed completely in its purpose because of lack of thoroughness. No scheme will succeed unless its final details are carried through.

Check the small details

Colin Powell, a professional soldier and US Secretary of State, relates a telling tale. He was on a course, jumping with others from a helicopter in the dark. Over the noise of the helicopter he yelled to the men to check their static lines that automatically opened their chutes when they jumped. Then, describing himself to be like a fussy woman, he checked them himself, including that of a sergeant, only to find that it was loose — something that the officer in charge, the jump-master, should have checked. His conclusion was 'never neglect details, even to the point of being a pest. Moments of stress and fatigue are exactly when mistakes happen. And when everyone else's mind is dulled or distracted the leader must be doubly vigilant. "Always check small things" was becoming another of my rules."[2] Your failure to check small details will not have such life-threatening consequences but it will have equal ability to threaten success.

Continually review priorities and stick by them

Initial priorities may not always be priorities later on and progress may be hindered through failure to appreciate this. Whatever function you are fulfilling at any given moment, you ought — without requiring time for thought — to be able to state the matters you recognize should have precedence in the use of your time and energies. Without this ability, you will lose sight of the essential through attention to the immediate. Efficiency requires the important to have precedence over the immediate for the latter may be only a minor issue. If you do not initiate and review matters efficiently, it is difficult for anyone else to do it.

Be prepared to learn

Be ready to learn anything that will improve your efficiency. Cultivate an open mind when suggestions are made. Gladly acknowledge your indebtedness to those whose ideas help you. Be concerned for effectiveness rather than superficial neatness and tidiness in methods and equipment. Nate Saint, a missionary pilot, looked at flying his plane from the point of view of efficiency and his words apply to many activities. 'We make sure that we don't carry anything in the airplane that isn't necessary. When our mission bought the plane, it had nice soft seats in it. But we found that these seats weighed almost eight pounds each. So we decided to use harder seats that weighed only one pound, and take seven pounds of extra food and cargo. On the wheels of the plane there were nice stream-lined fenders — or pants as they call them. They looked very nice but inside they were full of heavy mud. We decided to take them off. You know, lots of things are like that — they feel nice, or they look nice but they don't help us to get the job done. They hold us back, so we need to get rid of them.'[3]

Be prepared to admit an experiment a failure

No one succeeds without experimenting. If something does not work, do not be ashamed or try to cover it up. Simply ask the questions, 'Where and what next? What do we learn from what has happened and how do we move forward?'

Be prepared to seek advice when in doubt

Even if people expect you to know all the answers, you never will, and God certainly does not expect you to do so. Never feel it is beneath you to seek advice from those who have more knowledge in a sphere relating to your responsibilities. They will think none the less of you for asking their counsel; in fact, they will probably think more of you. Unwillingness to ask for help will make you inefficient where you could be much better equipped.

Remember people are more important than things

Thor Heyerdahl, Norwegian explorer, anthropologist and author, served with the Norwegian forces in World War II. He wrote, 'Few men with stripes and stars on their uniforms were admired by us enlisted men. I only remember two. The camp commander, Colonel Ole Reistad, was one. From him I learned that respect of a subordinate can be maintained and even increased by giving orders in such a way that the one who receives them still feels that he is an equal as a human being.'[4] William Temple, a twentieth-century Archbishop of Canterbury, gave valuable advice: 'The times when people's feelings are most sensitive are … the times when the greatest care is called for, both as a matter of policy and also a matter of charity.'[5] The maintenance of good personal relationships is a top priority. As a leader you must know and recognize what people's anxieties are and address yourself to dealing with them with sensitivity.

Be available

Avoid remoteness. Ensure that people do not think that you have office hours out of which they are not permitted to approach you. A good headteacher is seen all around the school, and in the staff room, so regularly that both staff and young people may easily seize an opportunity to talk with him or her if they want. A good army commander will often walk a deliberate route each day through the barracks so that he may be waylaid by those desperate to communicate with him. As the pastor of a church, I had a regular time each week with interview slots for those who wished to make appointments; but, far more importantly, I always shook hands with people at the end of meetings and remained behind to chat. Invariably people took the opportunity to raise something that was bothering them. It enabled me to keep my ear to the ground and to show my concern for people.

Beware of ruthless efficiency

Efficiency for efficiency's sake will make you cold and critical of people's mistakes. Rather than inspiring them to greater endeavour, you will paralyse them into inactivity through their fear of making blunders that will spark criticism. Basic to this avoidance of ruthless efficiency is ensuring that people have time to rest and relax. Anxious as Ezra was to get on with the important commission Artaxerxes had given him in Jerusalem, the record tells us: 'So we arrived in Jerusalem, where we rested three days' (Ezra 8:32). As a leader ensure that after activity people have adequate rest and time to themselves. This will not hinder; rather it will enhance their activity.

Efficiency is helped by incentives

Be generous in letters of appreciation and expressions of commendation. Do not be grudging in your praise or destructive in criticism. Give praise where it is due; and in giving criticism, as at times you must, do it constructively so that the person criticized wants to do better next time.

Relax!

Have other interests that provide relaxation and are a good use of your own times for rest. Most leaders tend to be workaholics and that is understandable because you may always be on call and responsibility often rests uniquely with you. But that makes a regular day off and times of relaxation all the more important. Even as the mind affects the body so too the body affects the mind. In fulfilling leadership duties you may be under both mental and emotional tension without realizing it. If you do not deliberately provide times for the release of your unconscious stress you will be imposing even greater strain upon yourself.

A relaxing interest that you can pick up and put down again easily is as important as your day off. A new bishop was about to take up his responsibilities and was invited to lunch by his senior bishop together with another who was about to retire. The senior bishop asked the retirement bishop, 'There's David over there starting out on being a bishop. What advice would you give him?' Without a moment's hesitation he replied, 'When I first became Bishop of Kingston, I thought that I must give up all my other commitments in order to be completely free for the parishes. It was a great mistake. You should keep other interests going.'[6] The important factor in such interests is that they should provide genuine relaxation and activity in a way different from our daily routine. For one person it may be renovating 'clapped-out' Volvo cars and for another bird-watching.

Personal efficiency

Quiet personal efficiency on your part will go far in establishing people's confidence in you. Do not talk too much about efficiency; instead, try to be a model of it. Never urge people to be competent; rather demonstrate to them the means whereby they may do to greater effect and profit what they already strive to do. If you can achieve this, your leadership will be invaluable. Few are able to accomplish this without effort; but you are not to expect that everything will come easily to you. 'If you are a leader, *exert* yourself to lead' (Romans 12:8, NEB).

Prayer

Heavenly Father, thank you that because you know and understand me perfectly your expectations of me are neither too high nor too low. Help me to have high standards for the work you have entrusted to me but gentleness and thoughtfulness in encouraging others to have similar standards. May I lead most of all by humble and unconscious example. I ask this for my Saviour's sake. Amen.

Questions for Bible study groups

Read Luke 14:25-35; Philippians 3:3-10; Romans 15:14-22; Romans 16

1. *Luke 14:25-35:* Jesus did not give the two illustrations of the person building a tower and the king thinking of going to war to teach principles of leadership but rather the importance of counting the cost of discipleship. However, the illustrations do have lessons to teach us about leadership. What are they?
2. *Philippians 3:3-10; Romans 15:14-22:* Paul identified the priorities he shared with all Christians and those that God had especially given to him. What were the former and what were the latter?
3. People are more important than things. In what ways does the last chapter of Paul's letter to the Romans illustrate that truth?
4. In what areas can you improve your personal efficiency?

Questions for church leaders

1. *Are we efficient in preparation and organization?*
2. *Are we putting off any difficult decisions?*
3. *Do we review our priorities with sufficient regularity and are we sticking by them?*
4. *Are we still eager to learn anything that will make us better equipped?*
5. *Is it obvious to our membership that people matter to us more than things?*
6. *Are we ready and willing to be available to people?*

10.
Colleagues

Seldom are we leaders in isolation; leadership is normally shared. We need to work well with others. That does not mean that they have to be exactly like us in temperament and gift. Different leadership styles can complement each other to everyone's benefit. Very different people can work effectively together whereas people who are very similar may find it hard to do so.

Basic to our success in working together is the building of a leadership team. This does not happen quickly. Rather, it requires patience, thought, prayer and hard work. Essential to that team will be a regular team meeting to which you in particular must give priority. As you do so, you may then expect all the team members to do the same. If for some legitimate reason a member of the team cannot be present, it is worth considering altering the date to ensure maximum attendance. To do that will underline your view of its importance, without you having to say so. The reason for aiming at a full attendance is that if a meeting is to be more than simply fixing dates and making practical arrangements, everyone needs to be there when you struggle with difficult issues and determine the way ahead. If someone is absent from an important discussion, he or she may get out of step with the others. If as the leader of the team you do not give this kind of lead it is virtually impossible for anyone else to do so.

If it falls to you to recruit members of a team, choose the best. What I have in mind here is the sad possibility that we may fail to appoint certain individuals because we feel that their gifts are superior to our own and that perhaps they may threaten us.

You may be a foundation member of the team or someone brought in when the team is well established. Your aim must be to complement the variety of gifts that are present. Although you are all very different people, you have to learn to work well together so that you form a harmonious unit. It would not do for you all to have the same gifts; your differences are vital to your contribution.

Leaders must know how to think and act towards their colleagues so that they work in harmony. The relationship of committee member to committee member, church council member to church council member, elder to elder and deacon to deacon needs thought and understanding. What we have to say in this chapter will apply to a far wider field than the local church, but we shall find our task easier if we limit the application of our principles to that sphere.

No church can run beyond its leaders; no church may be expected to do more than its leaders. Thus in all their busyness and activity leaders should not neglect their relationships with one another. The harmony of leaders is the key to the unity found within the local church. Leaders should set such an attractive standard that those who follow their direction want to be like them and to work with them.

Know your colleagues at every possible level

Know them well

You may feel that you are so involved with the fulfilment of your duties that you cannot really spare time to get to know your colleagues. If this is the case, you should not abandon the effort, but rather be more determined to do something practical about it. Not knowing well those you work with is a point of weakness that perhaps only a crisis may reveal. Even as Jesus recognized the individual temperaments of those working with him — for instance, calling James and John the Sons of Thunder (Mark 3:17) — take the trouble to recognize the varying characters and interests of those who work alongside you. Where it is possible, utilize their strengths and avoid exposing their weaknesses. From the moment a patient steps into a doctor's consulting room, a good doctor observes the patient. What he sees may be as important as what he hears or discovers on examination. Think of your colleagues one by one, not with the aim of being critical, but of recognizing where there are observable weaknesses and strengths, even as you yourself possess. When you are away from leadership meetings and have the opportunity to talk with them, discover their interests and establish a good personal rapport with them.

On the spiritual level

The deeper our personal fellowship with God, the more concerned we are for fellowship with colleagues. Nothing draws us closer together than praying together. Make a point of never discussing any important matter without concluding by praying together for God's help and blessing. We often get to know people best by praying with them. A regular meeting set aside for prayer will do much to strengthen relationships and fellowship in Christ.

Share their experiences

We tend to be much too silent about things that really matter, notably God's personal dealings with us. The frank opening of the heart between leaders provides spiritual refreshment that leaders may so easily lack through the obligation laid upon them to be giving out so much, with little opportunity sometimes of receiving. If our colleagues seem reluctant to share their experiences, we should take the initiative by sharing our own, for true fellowship can never be one-sided. Aim to develop a genuine love for colleagues, and fellowship will follow.

There will be important moments in their lives that we need to share with them if we can. They are as ordinary in their emotions as we are, and love their families as we do.

Deal with the first signs of disharmony

Deal immediately with any issue that seems to threaten harmony. We are out of touch with the real world if we imagine that there will never be any trace of such a problem in our sphere of service! A collection of people from different backgrounds and spheres of employment are bound to possess a variety of views and opinions. This diversity is not in itself harmful; however, it becomes damaging when individuals fail to adjust their views through stubbornness and self-will. Disagreement may arise quickly and surprisingly on issues that we would never have anticipated giving trouble. Do not try to hurry such issues through or pretend they do not exist, for in doing so you are bound to make matters worse.

Be positive in your contribution

Emphasize your twofold assurance that everyone wants what is right and that God is willing to give you corporate guidance. Perhaps you may be able to suggest that someone present, who appears to be neutral on the particular issue and whom you know to be respected by everyone, should come prepared at your next meeting to lead a discussion upon the matter, giving the pros and the cons.

Do not gloss over disharmony

To gloss over disharmony is always dangerous. It is like putting a coat of gloss paint over damp woodwork; the immediate appearance may look all right, but the dampness eventually reveals itself, causing damage to all that has been done. Deal with every evidence of disharmony in the atmosphere of prayer; and make the starting point of discussion what the Bible has to say by way of direct instruction or of principles to be applied.

Beware of exclusive friendships

Avoid exclusive friendships with any of your colleagues. Not all will be happy at this advice but caution over special friendships within a leadership team is wise. Quite unintentionally, special relationships may become an underlying cause of division or disagreement. If you encourage a particular friendship with a colleague, you may find yourselves discussing matters that are to be raised with those who share leadership with you. The result will be that when you meet in conference, for example, you will sometimes give the impression that your minds are made up and that you expect others to fall in with you.

Furthermore, if you have a special relationship with colleagues, you may feel bound to take sides with them, in debate or in a vote, out of loyalty rather than out of concern for common good. This does not apply, of course, when you share the leadership with just one other person; but where this is not the case, you should endeavour to be on equal terms of friendship with all.

Never deal with an important matter with only a small group of colleagues when it is possible to call all of them together to determine appropriate action. Do not allow yourself to be influenced by your estimate of the individual abilities of your colleagues in deciding with whom you should confer. If people are colleagues, you should treat them as such and not discriminate between them and others who seem to have better judgement. Recognize that people possess diverse capabilities and capacities and must not be judged by that very fallible standard — yourself. To deal with a matter in a small group when it ought to have been brought before a larger group sows seeds of disharmony, besides showing a lack of confidence in others.

Never act independently of your fellow leaders except where it is your clear duty to do so.

Be loyal and committed to your colleagues

Nothing enhances team spirit more than loyalty and commitment. Inevitably individual leaders will be subject to criticism. At such times they will feel vulnerable and discouraged. You will probably know whether the criticism is justified or not. Your loyalty will be shown as you endeavour to calm the words and actions of the criticizer and then speak honestly and graciously with the person criticized. While you may sense or be aware that the criticism voiced has some justice behind it, it is always appropriate to say to the critic, 'Remember, it is not easy to be in leadership and we all have our faults. Have you spoken to the person concerned? If not, why not do so?' Then and there pray with the person for the colleague who has been criticized and for wisdom to do the right thing. At the same time you will help the situation by talking to your colleague about the issue, showing that your honesty does not arise from blanket acceptance of the criticism but from your loyalty and commitment to helping him and your hope that he would do the same for you in similar circumstances. Go out of your way to encourage him and let him know how important he is to the team. In this way the person who deserves to be criticized is helped to put things right and the person who does not deserve to be criticized is not stumbled by it.

Leading leaders

There has to be a leader among leaders. Through what may be a twisted concept of Christian equality, people may sometimes suggest that such is unnecessary. Bitter experience proves them wrong. Tracy Edwards captained the first all-woman crew in the Whitbread Round-the-World Yacht Race in 1989 — a seemingly impossible achievement before the event. One of her hardest decisions was when she had to ask her most experienced crew member to leave. In her autobiography she writes, 'Cutting her loose had nothing to do with her seamanship. It came down to a power struggle that had been brewing ever since … we argued over tactics. There had seemed to be two skippers … which confused the crew and tested their loyalty unnecessarily.'[1] Do not be vague yourself or encourage others to be vague as to the precise responsibilities you and they have when leadership issues have to be decided.

I have known several situations where churches have experienced very encouraging growth so that as a result they have been able to call a second or even third minister. But then in some cases a mistake has been made. Rather than give one of them seniority — not that I like that term — they have determined that there should be absolute parity. With this in mind, they have removed the responsibility of chairmanship of leaders' meetings and church meetings from these men. Because their roles were not properly defined and their relationship to each other not established, conflict then arose between them and the other leaders so that eventually both men were in effect dismissed, with disastrous and lasting consequences for the men and their families and the church. There must be a leader among leaders. It is not so much a matter of seniority but the necessity for knowing who should take the initiative if there is any doubt in a situation.

If you are called upon to be a leader amongst leaders particular responsibility rests upon you for harmonious relationships. Regard yourself as a pastor to your colleagues. While they may have heavy responsibilities in the spiritual care of others, they themselves often need help — as also do you. Give of yourself to them, knowing that if by so doing you are able to help them, they will be enabled to help others much more effectively.

Discourage colleagues from talking about one another in your presence. Whenever an adverse opinion is expressed never readily agree, but instead say something positive and good about the colleague whose name has been raised. Deter colleagues from talking privately about an issue that is to come up for corporate discussion. Some will try to do this; but such conversation should be discouraged for it may easily lead to cliques that in turn lead to misunderstanding or division. When someone gives you special information, ensure that same information is given to all who are entitled to receive it. Be on your guard lest a colleague is passed over by the others.

As a leader amongst leaders, you will probably have to chair many leaders' meetings. Be careful to draw out each person's contribution and listen carefully. Make a practice of getting a different person in rotation to start the discussion on a fresh topic. Never allow a decision to be made if you do not feel that all have expressed their honest feelings. Draw out more retiring members and encourage the silent to speak. Postpone any decision that threatens to divide, and give time for prayer. Try to move forward by conviction rather than by influence. Learn to hold back from entering too much into discussion yourself — especially if you are a forceful person, as you probably are as a leader amongst leaders — so that others express their minds.

Make sure that your fellow leaders know that you do not mind them challenging your convictions and decisions. William Cooper was Assistant Deputy Director to Hudson Taylor in China. 'I don't like to oppose you so often,' he said to Taylor on one occasion in the early days of the China Council. 'I think I had better resign.' 'No, indeed!' replied Taylor. 'I *value* such opposition: it saves me from many a mistake.'[2] Hudson

Taylor recognized the value of creative tension. At the same time, having allowed free discussion, including critical debate, once the debate ends and a decision is made, all should see the decision through as if it were their own.

It is worthwhile repeating the value of meeting regularly for prayer; and as a leader amongst leaders it is up to you to see that pressure of business does not force it out. One of the reasons why the apostles practised delegation was that they wished to give more time to prayer (Acts 6:4). Do not scorn the idea of suggesting that you should spend a day a year relaxing together, perhaps arranging an outing of some sort, so that you may see one another as individuals rather than only as leaders.

When leaders know genuine oneness and spiritual fellowship in Christ, they find even the time and attention they give to business a means of spiritual refreshment. Tremendous spiritual uplift and encouragement can come to leaders through the fellowship they enjoy as they deal with the affairs of our Lord Jesus Christ's church. Do not be satisfied until this is the case.

Prayer

Father in heaven, I thank you for all the colleagues you have given me in the responsibilities entrusted to me. May our fellowship together be warm, stimulating and honouring to our Lord Jesus Christ. Help me every time we meet to be positive in my contribution, to be willing always to receive help from them but determined always to be as helpful as I can to them. I ask this in the name of our Lord Jesus Christ. Amen.

Questions for Bible study groups

Read Acts 15:36-41; Galatians 2:11-21; John 15:9-17

1. *Acts 15:36-41:* The disagreement between Paul and Barnabas was clearly an unhappy experience for both of them. What may we learn from it?
2. *Galatians 2:11-21:* Paul's opposition to Peter at Antioch was another sad incident. What were the grounds upon which Paul challenged Peter? What evidence is there that it was ultimately appreciated? (See, for example, 2 Peter 3:15.)
3. *John 15:9-17:* The Lord Jesus Christ called his disciples his friends because everything that he learned from his Father he made known to them (v. 15). As you think of all that you know of his ministry and teaching, what important lessons did he teach about working together? (Verses 12 and 17 provide one important starting point.)
4. As you review your experience of working with others, what has helped you most to work effectively together?

Questions for church leaders

1. *Do we know each other well enough? If not, what steps can we take to improve our knowledge?*
2. *Do we share with one another on the spiritual level as much as we ought?*
3. *Are there exclusive friendships that obtrude themselves and spoil our harmony?*
4. *Do we recognize a leader among leaders?*
5. *Do we meet together for prayer as frequently as we ought?*

11.
Team leadership

Jesus' call of the first twelve disciples recognized the team concept. At the beginning they were probably unaware of all that they were being taught about working as a team. But basic to the manner in which they were to work and to serve their Master were their good relationships with one another and the ability to work together. All of them were in leadership training. What they heard Jesus teach about leadership they saw perfectly exemplified in his life. While they were all potential leaders, it soon became apparent who would be leaders among leaders.

As we read the Acts of the Apostles and the New Testament letters, we see how the apostles — and especially Paul, of whom we know most — worked in partnership and taught principally by example.

Teams take many different forms in Christian work even as they do in secular life, particularly in work and sport. In the local church there will be a leadership team — often the elders and/or the deacons. Within the church fellowship, in the various church activities, there will be leadership committees for the young people's work, for women's groups, for men's groups, for pastoral care, for planning evangelistic outreach, the care of the elderly and many others. The potential list is large.

If, therefore, we are to work effectively, we need to know how to function as leaders in a team.

A permanent principle

Although all on the team may be leaders, the team itself, as we have established earlier, requires a leader. This principle needs to be applied consistently since it is essential for progress and harmony. In the context of elders and/or deacons, for example, the obvious leader is the minister and, if there are several, the senior minister. If it is a leadership team for the young people's work, then one of their number needs to be recognized as leader. As soon as that person's identity is established you have someone who can take many necessary actions on behalf of the group without misunderstanding. Some of the matters we will now concern ourselves with are the natural province of the principal leader.

For the sake of directness and simplicity, I am now going to imagine that you are the recognized leader of the team of which you are part. That does not mean that the rest of this chapter is not relevant to you if you are not that person, and for two reasons. Firstly, you need to know what to expect from this individual and how you may support his or her leadership. Secondly, in the nature of things, as a leader you may well find yourself in that person's position in the future. Let me express the priorities in the form of exhortations or directives.

Establish the regularity of team meetings

A team cannot work well together unless it meets regularly. The pattern of meeting should be so regular and memorable that everyone knows when the next meeting will be, without looking at their diary. It may be on a weekly, two-weekly, monthly or two-monthly basis. If the members of the team spend the whole of their working week at their tasks, then probably a weekly meeting is the best pattern, perhaps meeting for lunch or over breakfast. If the leadership team relates to responsibility that people exercise in addition to their daily work, then the better pattern may well be monthly. It is preferable to meet for short meetings regularly than longer meetings irregularly. Team meetings should be the highlight of the week or month.

Be clear as to the purposes of team meetings

Five purposes are clear.

1. *Simply to keep in touch with one another.* There needs to be the opportunity for any member of the team to raise matters and issues that are of concern to them and in which they need the counsel or support of their colleagues. More often than not there are no such matters to raise, but it is important to provide the opportunity to do so. That is why regular meetings are vital.

2. *To encourage mutual concern and support.* Leadership always has its headaches and heartaches. More often than not we can cope with them but discouragement is a principal weapon of the enemy of our souls. The members of the leadership team cannot easily share their discouragements with those whom they lead — and probably should not do so at all — but they can share them with their fellow leaders. To be able to do so is more than halfway to their solution.

3. *To enjoy fellowship, especially in prayer.* As matters are shared and issues openly discussed, the most natural thing is to turn to God in prayer and to pray specifically for all that has been mentioned. Nothing is more beneficial to the team than praying together and nothing must be allowed to restrict it. The leader of the team must be responsible for maintaining this priority.

4. *To keep the team in harmony and working with the same aims.* Any collection of leaders working together, whether large or small in number, will reflect varying personality types, backgrounds and experience. They will all be subject to a variety of influences both within the church fellowship and outside of it. Your responsibility as leader is to talk frequently about your common aims and the priority of harmony together. If you sense disharmony in the group, then you must sort it out.

5. *To anticipate spiritual needs within the team and be proactive in endeavouring to meet them.* As you pray for the members of your team, God the Holy Spirit will frequently make you sensitive to the spiritual needs of individuals within it. Similarly, as you listen to people's contributions or observe their body language, you may pick up from them perhaps a sense of discouragement or frustration. You may then at the close of the meeting perhaps say, 'Why don't we meet for coffee one morning soon?' or give the person a ring at home later with that end in view. This leads us naturally to our next directive.

Be a pastor to all the members of your team

All need pastoral care, including you. As the team leader, your task is not simply administrative but spiritual. Hopefully, because of your encouragement and example, all will feel a spiritual responsibility for one another, but it is your special responsibility.

You may exercise this privilege in a number of ways and they are all important. First, pray for each leader by name every week, endeavouring as you do so to enter into the personal situation of each, both in family and work responsibilities. Sometimes it may be an encouragement to be able to say to one of them, 'I was praying for you today' and then to explain what you specifically asked God for them.

Second, make sure that there is a spiritual element to every team meeting. We have mentioned the importance of praying together. Linked with that is the value of reading a brief Bible passage and commenting upon it in a way that is relevant and meaningful to the group. For several years a team of which I was part all used the same Bible Reading programme and so it was helpful at every team meeting to share something from the Bible passage we had all read earlier in the day. It deepened our sense of fellowship and belonging together. Praying together will naturally flow from sharing in the Scriptures and they will helpfully inform and stimulate prayer.

When talking with individual team members, just as it is natural to ask how they are physically so it is right from time to time to ask how they are spiritually. Before doing this, however, it is essential that you check your own spiritual well-being and that you ask the question with tact and gentleness. If, however, you do not show care in this way, there is little likelihood that others will feel able to do so.

From time to time it may be helpful to suggest to the team that you all read the same Christian book, perhaps a chapter before each meeting, and then spend ten minutes or so discussing it together.

Confirm the principle of team loyalty and exemplify it

The Bible word used most to express loyalty is faithfulness. As the writer of Proverbs says, 'Many a man claims to have unfailing love, but a faithful man who can find?' (Proverbs 20:6). It is an invaluable quality in every area of life and not least in team membership.

Every team has a constituency that it serves and inevitably at some point members of the team will be criticized by those whom they serve. The criticizers may make the criticisms to other team members or to the team leader. While it is right to listen in most cases, it is not right to agree. That is not to say that you do nothing. If you sense that there is some truth in the criticism, you may suggest that the criticizer expresses the criticism directly to the person he is criticizing. Or, alternatively, you may say, 'Thank you for sharing with me. I think that the best thing is for me to share this with the person concerned.' If you know for a fact that the criticism is unjust you must say so. Whichever course of action is right, at the same time suggest that you pray there and then together for the person whose name has been raised. Working in a team, we owe it to one another to be faithful in this way. Not to do so sows seeds of division because it spoils relationships.

There will be times when it falls to a leadership team to make a corporate decision about a difficult matter of policy or practice. After time for reasonable discussion, you, as the leader of the team, must call for a decision to be made, seeking for a consensus. You may find yourself outvoted but membership of the team, whether as a team member or leader, means that thereafter the decision is 'yours' and you work and act by it.

Show your control of the situation

A team leader must be gentle, considerate and thoughtful towards all the team but at the same time be in control of the team's direction. This is not to suggest anything approaching a dictatorial attitude but rather doing what Paul says in Romans 12:8 of those whose gift and function is leadership or *governing*: 'let him govern diligently'. In other words, if your task is leadership, you are to go about it diligently, taking your responsibility seriously. You are not to be the kind of person who just lets things happen.

While others may not see the complete picture of what the team is doing, you must. While others may be preoccupied with only their personal contribution, you must be concerned for everyone's input. If others do not see the big picture of what you are aiming at as a team, you must. When others are indecisive about action, you must reason things out and suggest the way forward. If the team is not working in complete harmony, you must be the person who asks yourself why and sets to work to deal with the problem.

Ensure participation

Some team members will be quiet and others noisy. Some will have a lot to say and others perhaps too much. The larger the team the more difficult it is to ensure that everyone — and particularly the quiet and more reticent — shares properly in the discussions that take place. While some will always speak, you must watch out for those who seldom or never speak. It will be helpful to the group and to that individual if you address them in the team meeting by name and ask, 'What do you think about this matter?' Make it plain that everyone is welcome to contribute but never required to do so.

Encourage a sense of privilege

Paul urges the Colossians to remember the high honour that was theirs, 'It is the Lord Christ you are serving' (Colossians 3:24). The impact of that statement is all the greater when we appreciate that the people he particularly addresses are Roman slaves who had become Christians. Their human masters were probably unfair sometimes in their dealings with them and as slaves they could hardly call their lives their own. But the amazing truth was that no matter how unworthy their human master they could do their work, including the most humdrum task, with a tremendous sense of privilege and dignity for it was the Lord Jesus Christ they served.

It is a tremendous privilege to serve God's people and that is the task of the team and all its members. But sometimes God's people may give the team a rough time, perhaps through too high expectations or a lack of understanding of their difficulties. At such times the team can become grumpy and critical of God's people and be tempted to speak disparagingly of them or of certain individuals. Never indulge in such yourself and discourage the team from doing so. Rather, when you sense that the team is finding some of its tasks a drudgery and effort, deliberately point them to Scriptures that speak of the glory and dignity of our Lord Jesus Christ whom we serve, and remind them and yourself of the price that he paid for our salvation.

Prayer

Almighty God, thank you that in Christian service and leadership you place us in teams. If we are not a leader, help us not to be jealous of whoever has that responsibility but rather to be active and positive in our support. If we are a leader among leaders, grant us to have the mind of our Saviour and to serve them with humility and understanding. For Jesus Christ's sake, Amen.

Questions for Bible study groups

Read John 14:1-4; Colossians 3:22-25

1. This chapter has stressed the importance of loyalty or faithfulness. How did the Lord Jesus Christ show his loyalty and faithfulness to his disciples? (John 14:2 is one illustration.)
2. *Colossians 3:22-25:* What difference should our faithfulness to the Lord Jesus Christ make to our daily work?
3. What can we do to encourage ourselves to realize our privilege in serving the Lord Jesus Christ? Support, if you can, your suggestions with Bible verses or passages.

Questions for church leaders

1. *Do we meet with the right regularity?*
2. *Do we show pastoral care for one another?*

3. *Are we recognizing the importance of regarding corporate decisions as decisions to be regarded and spoken of as our own, even if left to ourselves we might have decided differently?*
4. *How real is our sense of privilege in our leadership responsibilities?*

12.
Chairmanship

Most leaders have to chair meetings from time to time and others do so regularly. Some are naturally better at it than others. But we can probably all improve our efficiency and usefulness in this sphere. Both the efficiency with which business is carried out and the enjoyment members of the committee experience in being together is very much influenced by the skill and competence of the chairman.

Preparation

A key word is preparation. A deputy speaker of the House of Commons at Westminster described the secret of a successfully chaired debate in three words: preparation, preparation and preparation!

A vital part of any kind of chairmanship or leadership of a meeting is preparation, not simply by drawing up an agenda but asking essential questions like:

- What is the purpose of the meeting?
- What ideally should be the end results?

- What could hinder the achievement of these goals?
- How long should the meeting last?
- What is an appropriate division of the time available?

These questions seem all too obvious and commonsense but they are easily neglected.

The committee

Most of us can remember committee meetings that have seemed endless and even pointless time-wasters. Determine in your mind that you will play your part in avoiding such a state of affairs. Drawn-out meetings become a burden. Before ever the meeting begins, think through what needs to be accomplished and as it proceeds keep a firm hold on the reins.

One of your first purposes in chairing a committee must be to see that the subjects on the agenda are in a proper order of priority and importance so that if you find time running out and you have to draw the meeting to a close before arriving at the last items on the agenda no serious damage has been done. With this end in view, you may find it helpful to prepare the agenda by having slips of paper upon which you place each item that is to be raised. Then move them around to establish an appropriate order before writing out or typing the final agenda.

Basic to the agenda will be what can be described as *the opening worship* or *devotions* as the Scriptures are read and prayer offered. If the committee is small it is valuable if all pray, even if briefly. If the committee is large, then it is helpful to suggest that four or five pray and that you will close the prayer time by praying yourself.

Your second purpose must be to ensure that every subject on the agenda is adequately dealt with. This can be achieved only as appropriate time is allowed for it. It may be helpful to pencil in against the items on your copy of the agenda the ideal time to spend. Maintaining the proper tempo in a meeting is vital to achieving the proper ends. Only the chairman is in a position to keep the tempo right so that things are kept moving.

Your third purpose is to make sure that everyone on the committee has the opportunity to speak. As you think of its members, you will know those who are shy or reticent and those who are the opposite! As you contemplate the various topics, it may be obvious that there are some people who ought to be asked to make a contribution if you find them remaining silent. They will be grateful to you for taking the initiative and the committee as a whole will benefit.

Your fourth purpose must be to try and discern the key issues that ought to be mentioned or raised under each subject. Jot down beforehand some appropriate headings on your agenda and then if they are not brought up introduce them yourself to the discussion. Sometimes it may be better to suggest at the beginning that certain important aspects should be considered as the subject is discussed.

Your fifth purpose must be to aim at unanimity and a deliberate seeking of God's will together. Aiming at agreement does not mean that there cannot be argument or debate since these are essential if questions are to be thoroughly and honestly aired and resolved. Sometimes in the middle of a debate it may be appropriate for you to remind your fellow committee members that the most important issue is not the achieving of your own will but discovering and doing God's will. If a discussion becomes overheated, nothing can be more beneficial than suggesting some moments of prayer together about the subject in hand. However there must come a point when as chairman you say that there has been sufficient discussion; a decision must now be made, and one that all will stand by even if it may not have been their personal choice.

William Temple was a popular Archbishop of Canterbury in the first half of the twentieth century. He was considered to be an unrivalled chairman. He allowed appropriate discussion and debate but 'the moment always arrived when he would rise and say, "I wonder whether something like this represents the sense of the meeting?", and his summing up would be so comprehensive of all the speeches that there was nothing more to be said.'[1] Endeavour to let all concerned present their views and positions, without interruption. Then let there be a free-for-all in which debate and argument can take place. But at an appropriate time take over, summarize all that has been said, and establish the consensus for action.

The church prayer meeting

Once again, preparation is the key. As its leader you need to ask yourself essential questions.

- What is the purpose of the prayer meeting?
- How may that goal be achieved?
- How long after its commencement should the people be praying?

Once more no apology need be given for establishing the obvious since that is what we often forget! The primary purpose of a prayer meeting is to pray and therefore preliminaries should be kept to the barest minimum. Where there are enough people to sing, there is undoubted value in usually beginning with a hymn or song of praise to God, especially when people come from a busy day at work and need to be helped in turning their thoughts to God in all his majesty and willingness to hear his people's prayers. A brief Bible reading and explanatory comment serve a similar purpose but the prayer meeting is not the place for a lengthy Bible reading and exposition.

As leader of the prayer meeting you must ask yourself further questions.

- What should the focus of our praying be?
- How should the time for prayer be divided up to fulfil this focus?

To give that focus you or someone else will need to provide helpful information to fuel and stimulate prayer. But the amount of information must not be so vast that it pushes out time for prayer. If someone other than yourself is to provide this information, you, as the leader, must tell that person how long he or she has and why you are restricting the time. It may often be better for you to ask him or her questions so that you may keep control of the time used.

Church business meetings

If you are leading a church business meeting, you must be involved in the preparation of the agenda so that it reflects the meeting's priorities. The minister, or senior minister, is the obvious and ideal person to lead church meetings. The church naturally and rightly looks to his leadership and as important as getting through business is ensuring that the meeting is a spiritual encouragement to everyone. Furthermore, church business should be done in the context of worshipping God and seeking his direction. The minister/pastor should carefully plan an opening act of worship, with a reading from the Scriptures that will direct everyone to the Head of the church to whom all are subject. Again, ask the right questions.

- What do we want to see achieved by this meeting?
- What are the most important matters that need to be dealt with or what are the issues to be resolved?
- What could hinder these purposes?
- What measures should we have in hand so that they are not hindered?

Once you have established the agenda, it will again help if you pencil in the amount of time you feel you should allow to be devoted to each item. Do not let this be a rod for your own back so that you feel a failure if you do not achieve it, but it will help you to keep the meeting going at the right pace to get through the agenda with a balanced use of time. Sometimes it is wise to tell people what you feel may be the right proportion of time to give to key items. As in preparing for a committee meeting, decide the factors that ought to be considered in any discussion so that if no one else raises them you can do so.

If a number of people are to make contributions — often some of your fellow leaders — tell them how long they have, and suggest that they write down what they want to say so that they can time themselves before the event. Both you and they will benefit by your suggesting that you meet for prayer immediately before the meeting begins. If you as leader do not do this, it is unlikely that anyone else will feel able to do so.

Be prepared for the unexpected! That is particularly relevant advice when it comes to that usually final matter on the agenda, 'Any Other Business'. When the date of the meeting is announced, it is entirely appropriate for you and your colleagues to ask people wishing to raise matters to give prior notice. If the question they raise is important, perhaps relating to policy or problems, you do not want to be taken unawares and especially at the end of a busy evening when many will want to get home. If the concern is genuinely important and ought to be raised, then you can place it earlier in the agenda. The last thing you want is for people to go home with a discordant note in their memories.

Sometimes, quite unexpectedly, because of questions asked as the meeting proceeds, you may become aware of tension or potential disagreement. It is helpful to have in readiness the announcement of a hymn or song that focuses attention on the person of our Lord Jesus Christ so that in singing it you will be consciously reminding everyone of his Headship and the importance of having his honour always in view.

Church services

More and more churches involve members of the church fellowship in the conduct of services, both on a Sunday and during the week. While the minister will probably do the teaching and preaching, someone else may lead the service, or pray, or read the Bible, or be responsible for the praise and music. There is much that is good in this but there are dangers. The first is that one person may not be in control of all that takes place. This is particularly the case when a minister hands over the music and the leadership of praise to musicians. What can sometimes happen then is that the musicians play what they enjoy playing or perhaps can play easily.

The second danger is that if people 'take turns' to lead and to contribute they may fall into the snare of feeling it to be the golden opportunity to do their own thing and perhaps go overboard in saying much more than needs to be said and end up drawing attention to themselves.

If you have the responsibility of leading a church service, key questions need to be asked.

* What should be included? What are the proper constituent parts?
* How do they fit with the Bible passage being read and preached?
* What is the appropriate order?
* Is there a place on this occasion for the involvement of others in the conduct of the service?
* If the answer is in the affirmative, how can that be achieved for the benefit of everyone?
* What practical features must be looked after?
* What is the ideal timing for the length of the service?
* What time should the preacher start preaching?

Remember, if you do not ask and answer these questions, no one else can do so and affect the outcome for good. Basic constituents for any service are praise, prayer, Bible reading and teaching. Praise will cover not only singing that is specifically an expression of praise to God but also the singing of biblical truth that encourages believers in their faith and walk with God. Bearing in mind that congregations are made up of people of all ages and the tremendous inheritance we have in our hymn and song books, a balance should be struck between the best of the old and of the new. There should not be such an emphasis upon singing that by the time God's Word is preached people are weary and tired.

Prayer is, of course, vital. The first main prayer in a service should always include adoration of God and thanksgiving to him. Very few people come to a service prepared in heart as we would want or they would choose. By such prayer we remind ourselves that we are in God's presence and why we have come together. The second main prayer should be one of intercession. The neglect of this in many services is serious — serious because it is commanded in the New Testament and because it means we fail to exercise our very special privilege as God's people. It also means that we fail to teach young Christians how to pray for they best learn by hearing older Christians praying.

The public reading of the Bible is vital. It helps to read the passage through carefully beforehand to ensure that you have the sense and know where the stress should be. Often it may be appropriate to have two Scripture readings, especially if it helps people to see how one serves to explain another.

When establishing the best order of the constituent parts, especially when there are perhaps some extra items, writing each part down on a separate piece of paper, and then juggling them around to establish the tidiest organization saves time and yields benefits.

If others are to be involved in leading (that is to say, being in the chair), or praying or reading, take that delegation seriously. Prepare intelligently with each person. With the leader, suggest how he should establish the right order and balance of things. If someone is going to take the opening prayer, put forward the most important aspects of that first prayer and recommend that they will find it helpful to either write it out beforehand or at least write down the main truths and desires they want to express. The same principle applies to the intercessory prayer. To suggest that people keep their eyes and ears open as they watch the TV news or hear the radio news programmes for matters of concern will help them to pray intelligently. Probably three or four main items for intercessory prayer are ideal.

Those who are reading the Bible should be encouraged to read it through carefully beforehand to ensure they understand what they are reading. The question of audibility is relevant to everyone's contribution and should be deliberately raised by you. In every group of people there will be those who are hard of hearing. Little is more frustrating for them than not to be able to hear and it is thoughtless and discourteous not to think of them. If people are taking part publicly for the first time it is wise to suggest that you meet before people arrive so that you may test out their voices and audibility.

If you are responsible for the overall leadership of a service do not allow things to move out of your control, especially with regard to the time given to music and the amount of singing. If you are responsible for delegating the leadership, never do so without giving clear instruction as to what is necessary. The best way of doing so is often by sharing, 'This is how I do it and I think you will find it helpful.' Everyone who has any responsibility in leading the service will be helped and encouraged by your suggesting that you should meet for prayer together before the service. When the service is over do not forget to commend what is good and suggest ways to improve anything that has fallen short.

Prayer

Heavenly Father, I confess that it is all too easy to speak glibly of doing things for your glory. Please pardon any glibness on my part and by your gracious Spirit help me to recognize and do what causes the name of the Lord Jesus to be held in high honour and for his people to be built up in their faith and obedience to him. For his name's sake. Amen.

Questions for Bible study groups

Read Acts 15:1-29; 1 Corinthians 14:26-40

1. *Acts 15:1-29*: Some might feel that debate should not be necessary. How did the early church resolve the difficult issue of what it should require of Gentile Christians? Are there principles we may learn from the spirit and conclusion of their discussion?
2. *1 Corinthians 14:26-40*: The NIV entitles this section 'Orderly Worship'. What important principles does Paul establish for orderly worship?

Questions for church leaders

1. *What instruction and direction do we give to people when we ask them to share in any public meeting or service?*
2. *Thankful for music and song, is that aspect of our worship under control?*

3. *Is the prayer meeting a highlight of the church's week?*
4. *How can we improve our meetings for church business so that they edify the membership and are something to which everyone looks forward?*

13.
Problems

All with any experience of leadership will recognize the appropriateness of the title of this chapter. Those who have little experience may imagine — being rather starry-eyed still about the whole matter — that leaders never have any problems. John Beames was an Assistant Commissioner in nineteenth-century India, which meant that he served as judge and deputy to the man who ruled the region. 'Governing men is grand work, the noblest of all occupations,' he wrote, 'though perhaps the most difficult.'[1]

Loneliness

If you follow the recommended practice of avoiding close friendships with those whom you lead or with one of your colleagues in leadership, you will sometimes find yourself lonely, with a sense of isolation.

To recognize that this is a common problem helps, because at least you know that you are not unique in the feeling. If you are married, much of the difficulty is solved, in that you have one person to whom you may open your heart and share most experiences. The help that may come from this relationship underlines the importance of the spiritual oneness of husband and wife already mentioned (chapter 3).

The support that comes from a marriage relationship may not, however, completely relieve the sense of loneliness; and the unmarried leader may be especially aware of the difficulty. If this is a problem, and it is not always so, deepen your relationship and friendship with any who are outside the immediate sphere of your work. It may be someone whom you meet in your daily employment or a friend whom you may meet from time to time or with whom you are able to speak on the phone. Most of us have someone to whom we may turn who is not directly involved in our responsibilities. Cultivate that friendship and recognize it to be God's gift.

Whatever happens, God can meet your problem of isolation when you experience it and even use it to throw you more upon his friendship. A particular aspect of loneliness in leadership arises when you recognize that you cannot readily share the secret fears you may have because you do not want to discourage others or sow similar fears in their hearts and minds. Trust in God and confiding in him, however, must be the first answer to your fears. Those fears may be used by him to deepen your faith and make you stronger in leadership.

Rigid self-discipline

You cannot lead others without sometimes being sorely provoked; you cannot get others working with you without knowing disappointment through inefficiency and failure. How many times you may feel that you want to let rip! Nevertheless, you should avoid this temptation; instead, you must learn to hold yourself back, keeping a steady check upon your feelings and tongue.

Many problems revolve around this question of self-discipline. While others may be at liberty to show their feelings, there will be many occasions when such freedom is not permitted you — either by others or by yourself. An indication of disapproval, for example, when people are talking to you about a difficulty may completely remove their confidence in you and make them feel that it is not worthwhile sharing with you. A thoughtless and hasty reaction may ruin a relationship that will take a long time to heal. While like others you may experience moments of panic when critical issues raise their head or hard decisions have to be made, you must not show your fear or allow yourself to be paralysed by it.

The main answer to this problem is to appreciate your vulnerability so that you are on our guard. Try to keep your feelings under control; never act in haste; make a habit of sleeping on any difficulty that arises. Above all, seek the help of your Master who when 'they hurled their insults at him, he did not retaliate; when he suffered, he made no threats' (1 Peter 2:23).

Indispensable

If you are able and efficient as a leader, there is a tendency for people to become so dependent upon you that they regard you as indispensable. Besides being bad for you, this belief is certainly unhelpful to them. No one is indispensable while our

Lord Jesus Christ is at the helm. John Owen, the seventeenth-century Puritan, wrote when he was near to dying, 'I am leaving the ship of the church in a storm; but whilst the great Pilot is in it, the loss of a poor under-rower will be inconsiderable.'[2]

A bishop of a former generation is said to have suggested that if you want to know how indispensable you are, you should stick your finger into a bowl of water and then withdraw it. The hole that will be left is the size of the vacancy that will be left by your passage from the scene! There is an element of exaggeration, of course, in that suggestion but the truth remains that no one is indispensable. God often has to teach us that humbling fact. An attack of pneumonia gave jungle-pilot Nate Saint time to think about the plans he had for his plane: 'The Lord used it to help me "let go" of the plane project,' he said. 'So easy for one to get feeling essential.'[3]

Much as your pride may enjoy the feeling it receives when people imply that they could not manage without you, you should aim at making yourself dispensable. Where possible, endeavour to have an understudy for every major task you do. Seek to achieve such a measure of delegation that, in your absence, affairs do not come to a standstill. Whilst having a finger upon everything, avoid having your hands on all that goes on! It is probably not a sign of failure for people to regard your services as indispensable but should they prove to be right because you have not taken steps to delegate, then you have failed in efficient leadership.

Misunderstanding

It is to be hoped that you will not be involved in misunderstanding, but there are occasions when it is inevitable. Moses found it to be so. Exodus 17 describes how 'the whole Israelite community set out from the Desert of Sin, travelling from place to place as the LORD commanded. They camped at Rephidim, but there was no water for the people to drink. So they quarrelled with Moses and said, "Give us water to drink." Moses replied, "Why do you quarrel with me? Why do you put the LORD to the test?" But the people were thirsty for water there, and they grumbled against Moses. They said, "Why did you bring us up out of Egypt to make us and our children and livestock die of thirst?"' Their response was totally unreasonable and unfair. But Moses responded in the right way. He 'cried out to the LORD, "What am I to do with these people? They are almost ready to stone me"' (Exodus 17:1-4). Like Moses, you must be ready to accept a lot of undeserved blame and fault-finding.

You may sometimes have to act in the light of facts that are known only to you — or perhaps also to your colleagues — which you cannot rightly divulge to others. Not knowing your private information, people may completely misjudge your actions; they may consider you unfair and unjust. Such criticism may be difficult to bear, for one of the last things you want is to be misunderstood. Yet you ought not to spring automatically to your own defence when such situations arise. There is a measure in which misunderstanding must be expected, for you will not always be able to explain the grounds on which you act. Having the mind of Christ in you, you will not cling to your rights and prerogatives (Philippians 2:6).

If ever you are misunderstood and it is within your power to explain to those involved the considerations that have moved you to act or speak, do, of course, seek the opportunity to do so, as soon as possible. However, where such would be indiscreet and your hands are tied by circumstances, you should bear the misunderstanding, learning to entrust yourself 'to him who judges justly' (1 Peter 2:23). Never be offended when you are misunderstood.

Involvement with problems

Leadership in the church inevitably means that individuals come to you with their problems, wanting help and guidance. Repeatedly you have to bear and share the burdens that others carry. This feature of your work brings the danger of over-involvement with people's difficulties. You may find yourself getting caught up personally and emotionally. Understandable as this is, it will do you no good and will prove detrimental to your effectiveness.

In dealing with people, you should give them all your attention and every sympathy of which you are capable. Whatever it is possible for you to do on the practical level, you should try to do. Then learn to draw the line, almost impossible as it may sometimes seem. Even as you encourage people to cast their burdens upon the Lord, you must learn to do precisely the same thing. You will be helped if you remember that problems come and go; and that few difficulties are as large and as impossible as they appear at first encounter.

As you look back over your experience so far, you will probably realize that you have been under stress and lost many hours of sleep over situations that really did not merit such anxiety, not least because God is always in control and it is his work that you do. You may be helped by the play on the words, 'It came to pass.' Difficulties do not last — they *pass*.

This whole question of personal involvement may be aggravated by the encouragement you give to people to depend upon you. Whilst it is good that you should encourage people to turn to you, your priority is to get them depending first upon God, and then looking to you as his servant.

Never off-duty

Few leaders can call time 'their own'. At any moment a needy individual may ring the doorbell or phone up. Snags may arise unexpectedly in delegated tasks that require immediate attention and those who work under your leadership need to feel that they may easily seek your help.

Although the principles stated in this chapter are appropriate, you need to have a private life and you require periods when you are 'off-duty'. No one can afford to be on the go all the time; your mind and body are incapable of working efficiently if they are not given opportunity to relax. You may wear yourself out by engaging in tasks that are too heavy for you as Moses did when he served as judge for the people from morning till evening without sharing and delegating the responsibilities (Exodus 18:13).

If you are not careful, you will find yourself at the disposal of everyone, with no time to yourself. The result will be decreasing efficiency, overtiredness and — since you are human — tendencies to self-pity and irritability.

Set aside times when you deliberately aim at relaxing, even though you may not be able to maintain them regularly. You owe it to your family and friends to do so, as well as to yourself. Make sure you take all your holidays because they will enhance your total efficiency. Try not to take work home with you if you work away from home. If you work at home, aim to close the door of your workroom or study at a regular time each day — and that will often be difficult. Expect and encourage your colleagues to do the same, especially when you have some jurisdiction over them.

Having laid down the principle, you are much more likely to achieve it than you would without having set goals. A hobby or profitable recreation is invaluable; but avoid a recreation that thoroughly exhausts or frustrates you if you are interrupted. If you feel that such times for relaxation just cannot be fitted in, you are wrong! All leaders need their 'Sabbath'.

Rebels

Much heartache will be avoided if you recognize that all leaders find the inevitable few who are 'against the government'. No matter how much you try to please them, you may find that they refuse to recognize your leadership or that they accept it very grudgingly. A biographer of Dawson Trotman, the founder of The Navigators, makes a significant comment about him: 'Though he delighted in the spiritual growth and development of his men, he paradoxically but humanly enough reacted when one rose to challenge his own leadership. It was an unrecognized chink in his armour that plagued him and cost him in later years.'[4] Seldom will you create a team without someone — often someone whom you have nurtured and encouraged — challenging you. Rather than regarding such people as rebels, respond positively. Then instead of being rebels they may become better colleagues.

Fortunately you need not worry too much about rebels for few will listen to them, for what they say about you they will almost certainly have said about your predecessors. The kind of 'rebels' of whom we write are recognized for what they are by discerning people, and the less discerning soon come to realize the inconsistency of their approach, so that what they say is ignored.

Your own attitude towards such people is important. Pray for them. Think the best of them; if you put the worst construction on what they do, you will remove any possibility of a changed attitude on their part. Overwhelm them with kindness. Give no legitimate cause for complaint in your dealings with them, although they may find unjustifiable causes nevertheless. Be quick to take them into your confidence, where it is right to do so. Kindness rather than hardness is the principle. To win over a rebel is a real achievement of leadership, although do not be too disappointed if you do not seem to be successful. The priority is that you should show the love of Christ to them.

Overfamiliarity

If you have grown up in a sphere of service, you may have the problem of people who are overfamiliar with you because of a past relationship when you were not in a position of leadership. You need to treat everyone in the same way and this necessarily means not being overfamiliar with anyone, especially in public. Some of your friends may not appreciate this attitude — or may deliberately choose not to understand it. They may be presumptuous and trade upon the former relationship.

You will be helped if you recognize what often lies behind this attitude: it is the fear that a former relationship will be lost through your 'elevation to office' and that you may not want to continue the previously enjoyed friendship. The situation will be helped, therefore, if you go out of your way to show that the relationship continues, and you are still the same person. When this has been established, it will not be long before you are able to speak about the problem, perhaps telling them that you do not want them to be embarrassed by the new circumstances. Then make the suggestion that when together in private you should act to one another as before. But point out the unhelpful impression that overfamiliarity could sometimes give to people who know nothing of your past relationship — a feeling of favouritism. It may be possible for a mutual friend to broach the matter if you feel it too difficult for you. Sometimes a problem like this has to be lived with; but do not give in to it without at first trying to rectify it in a sensitive way.

Disappointment

Hopefully leadership will be a happy task, but the Bible implies that there will be a fair share of pain and grief at times, not least over individuals (Hebrews 13:17). You will often find yourself crying to God, 'What am I to do with these people?' (Exodus 17:4).

When people first come into leadership, they usually do so with ambitious plans and visions of success, without ever considering the possibility of failure or difficulties along the way. Confirmed optimist, as you need to be, you should recognize also that disappointments are the particular lot of leaders. Sometimes the disappointments may be bitter and may destroy all that you have begun to build, and you may have to start all over again — although not quite 'all over again' for next time you should be able to profit from the hard lessons you learn in the school of experience.

To recognize the inevitability of disappointments where human nature is concerned is halfway to overcoming them. Whenever disappointment knocks you down, pick yourself up and determine, by God's help, to persevere. Problems will appear at regular intervals; effective leadership demands that the same problems do not exist a year later. It is faith that equates problems with success. 'Success is the ability to go from one failure to another with no loss of enthusiasm' (Winston Churchill).

Loss of vision

Loss of vision is seldom a problem to newly-fledged leaders, but it may be an urgent one for established ones, who have seen their initial aims and objects fulfilled. Vision accomplished should mean vision renewed; and yet so often that is not the case. The activity in which you are engaged can become so much part of you and you so much part of it, that instead of remaining the leader you become part of a piece of machinery that is never overhauled. It may then continue to grow and develop without anyone calling a halt to ensure that the direction in which everything is going is satisfactory and effective.

No matter how busy they are, leaders need to fit into their programme periods when they get away from their sphere of responsibility for a while, so that they may try to review it as a whole and gain an understanding of God's will for the future. Where leadership is shared, all who have leadership responsibility should endeavour to get apart together. If church councils, elders, deacons, committees, mission leaders and the like give time to standing back and endeavouring to see situations as a whole, lethargy will be avoided and dispelled since vision is a principal answer to it. If you lose your vision, cry to God for its renewal.

These problems, and many others that could be mentioned, all underline the importance of a call from God to leadership.

Without a clear call from God, those in Christian leadership either become quickly disheartened or lower their standards, doing only those things that they find enjoyable. If, however, you are sure that your call is from God, every problem is a challenge to faith, and such a challenge is always a means of blessing, both for you personally and for those whom you lead.

Prayer

Holy Father, I recognize that the reality and proof of my call to any task that you give me is my persistence and continuance in it. Help me to recognize that problems and difficulties are inevitable in a fallen world where the enemy of our souls is always at work. Grant that I may see these challenges as opportunities to trust you and may I prove to be more than conqueror through my Saviour, the Lord Jesus Christ. For his name's sake. Amen.

Questions for Bible study groups

Read Exodus 17:1-7; Hebrews 13:7-17

1. *Exodus 17:1-7:* What particular problems of leadership does this passage reveal?
2. What were the serious implications of the people's actions towards Moses?
3. *Hebrews 13:7-17:* Verses 7 and 17 identify a number of good leadership qualities. What are they? What is the appropriate response of God's people to such leadership?

4. When responsibility for others has been yours, what problems have you encountered? What answers have you found?

Questions for church leaders

1. *What will help us when we feel isolated or lonely in our leadership?*
2. *If we are married, are there limits to what we may properly share with our marriage partner?*
3. *How may we safeguard our times with our families?*
4. *Are there those whom we may think of as rebels? How may we act positively towards them?*
5. *Which of the suggested problems registers most with us?*

14.
Perils

This chapter and the previous one may seem somewhat ominous and frightening in their titles. To read of problems and of perils is not exactly encouraging! Nevertheless, it is imperative that you face up to the responsibility of leadership that both these chapters indirectly stress. If anyone needs to have a due sense of responsibility, it is the Christian leader. The Gospels show how hypocrisy, for example, was a peril for the religious leaders of the day. No doubt some of their number must have warned them against it. An understanding of problems before they arise and of perils before they become realities is indispensable for the responsible discharge of your duties. It is time to give attention now to some of the perils of leadership.

Leading people astray

It is a fact of human life that what is good may be turned to what is evil; that what has the highest potential for the benefit of others may also have the greatest possibilities for evil. The gift you have for leadership may be used to the profit of many, but used wrongly it can be disastrous and evil in its consequences. To be a recognized guide of others and to lead them astray and confuse them is to be worthy of condemnation (Isaiah 3:12; 9:14-16). When a big tree falls, lots of little ones fall with it.

The apostle Peter had, by his leadership, been an example to the Galatian Christians, but, through fear of people, he compromised, with the result that others followed him and were led astray (Galatians 2:11-14). Paul had to withstand Peter to his face, for he was clearly in the wrong. Having followed Peter in the good example he gave, Galatian Christians found themselves almost automatically following him in his bad example.

When Peter exhorted the elders of scattered churches throughout Asia Minor to be 'examples to the flock' (1 Peter 5:3), he probably had in view the warnings Jesus gave about leading others astray, as well as the lessons he had learned from bitter personal experience.

A false stewardship

It is a dreadful responsibility to use the gift of leadership wrongly. Better never to have the gift than to possess it and use it amiss.

In encouraging his readers to give heed to their leaders, the writer to the Hebrews reminds them that their leaders watch for their souls 'as men who must give an account' (Hebrews 13:17). If God gives much, then much is required (Luke 12:48). Leadership faithfully exercised has its special reward; leadership sinfully used has its special condemnation.

Paul's watchfulness against false stewardship was seen in his endeavour to live and act continually as 'in the sight of God'

(2 Corinthians 4:2). He tried to have his actions influenced by his knowledge of the certainty of the coming judgement (2 Timothy 4:7-8). Peter seems to suggest that as a stimulus to a conscientious stewardship of their gifts and responsibilities Christian leaders should always bear in mind the return of the Chief Shepherd (1 Peter 5:4).

Conceit and pride

One of the reasons for discouraging young Christians from assuming a position of responsibility in the church too quickly is human proneness to pride (1 Timothy 3:6). Mature Christians are no less vulnerable to conceit than the recent convert. While you may tend to shrink in size with age your ego does not. However, you should be more ready to recognize the rearing of pride's ugly head and should know better how to deal with it. Hudson Taylor, founder of the China Inland Mission (now Overseas Missionary Fellowship), was introduced to a congregation in Melbourne, Australia, as 'our illustrious friend'. 'Dear friends,' he began, 'I am the little servant of an illustrious Master.'[1] You may spoil the good work you do by allowing yourself to take the credit for it.

One form of leadership leads to another; and some spheres bring public prominence. In a less public position you may not have found humility too much of a problem, yet a major responsibility may reveal truths about your proud heart that you have not before realized. Great help is found in turning to Bible passages — such as James 4:6-10, beginning with the words, 'God opposes the proud but gives grace to the humble' — that deal with this issue and then making the teaching of Scripture on humility the substance of your prayer. Even greater help is found in deliberately thinking of the example of our Lord Jesus and the teaching he gives that our purpose is never to be to lord it over others but to serve them — even to be their slave (Mark 10:42-44).

The obligation is laid upon you not to think of yourself more highly than you ought to think (Romans 12:3). Take note of wise sayings that cut you down to size like, 'Accept that someday you're the pigeon and someday you're the statue' (source unknown). Another such statement is that made by Abraham Lincoln when he was informed by a telegraph operator at the War Department that the Confederates had captured a bunch of horses and a Union brigadier general. 'The operator was surprised when Lincoln expressed more concern over the horses. Lincoln supposedly explained, "I can make a brigadier general in five minutes. But it's not so easy to replace one hundred and ten horses.'[2] It was said of Silvio Conte from Massachusetts, an American Republican senator in the 1950s, that the secret of his success was 'that he took most issues seriously but he never took himself seriously'.[3]

If you find you are beginning to believe you are indispensable or are enjoying other people considering you so, you should immediately look round and attempt some sensible delegation of responsibility. Leaders meet many who flatter them; never fall into the mistake of imagining that these are your best friends! It is better to hear the rebuke of the wise than to listen to the praise of fools (Ecclesiastes 7:5). A constructive critic will help much more than an unthinking admirer. If the former pricks your bubble of pride, thank God — painful as the pricking may be. Arrogance is incompatible with love (1 Corinthians 13:4); love does not put the worst interpretation upon a criticism.

Pride is a continual snare for leaders at all stages of their leadership. The writer of 2 Chronicles makes a succinct and telling comment about King Uzziah: 'But after Uzziah became powerful, his pride led to his downfall' (26:16). God may choose to 'exalt' a leader in the sight of those whom he leads and they may properly 'revere' him, as in the case of Joshua (Joshua 7:14). But if ever the leader takes credit for it or uses it to manipulate God's people then it is abused. The best things are always capable of abuse.

A domineering attitude

With pride comes the peril of dictatorship. Leadership brings the obligation of directing people and of giving instructions. You may enjoy this too much; you need to be careful therefore that you do not become a little dictator.

Christian leadership is not lordship. Peter warns elders against tyrannizing the flock of God (1 Peter 5:3). You may become so used to laying down principles and giving instructions that almost unconsciously you become a law to yourself. Those who think they alone are right and can never be wrong are in a perilous position. The peril is avoided as you recognize that you are to lead by example rather than by dictation and pressure. Any desire to make people bend their wills to yours is contrary to the biblical pattern. Those who domineer have forgotten that they are answerable to the Chief Shepherd. Wise leaders exercise authority without assertiveness.

A lack of accountability

Leaders must never be a law to themselves. They must not fall into the snare of pastoring others without recognizing their own need of pastoral care. They are no less likely to fall into error or moral danger than those for whom they care. Their proneness may be all the greater because the enemy of their souls makes them his special target.

No easy answers to the problem of accountability can be given but it needs to be aimed at with integrity. It is especially relevant if you are in leadership on your own and if people tend to idolize you. If that is the case, it will help if you can find someone of maturity, whom you trust, outside your immediate sphere of service with whom you can meet regularly, say at three-monthly intervals, and who may be relied upon to ask you the right questions about your relationship to God and manner in which you lead.

If you lead with others, you need to cultivate a genuine openness about your relationship to God and a deliberate commitment to each another to raise privately any concern you may feel about each other's attitudes or behaviour.

Possessiveness

The refusal to let go of a sphere of responsibility has done as much to hinder the effectiveness of Christian churches and organizations as any other peril mentioned in this chapter. 'This job is mine and no one else is going to lay their hands upon it' can be the unspoken attitude.

An element of possessiveness is understandable. For example, if you have been involved in an activity since its beginning and have seen it grow, you will naturally be glad, and inclined to regard it as your work. You will be afraid of anyone taking it over who may spoil what has been already achieved. Even so, this kind of possessiveness has its dangers. You will be able to deal with this peril if you appreciate its underlying mistakes. Those who are possessive in this way forget that the work is God's, rather than theirs. Whatever success they have found comes from God. To say that is not to fail to appreciate the hard work and industry of these leaders, but if they are spiritual people they will recognize that all true progress comes from God. Possessive leaders probably feel that no one else can do the job as well as they do it; and this is a delusion. God is able to equip others, even as he has present leaders.

Possessive leaders kill the very work they want to perpetuate: they quench the enthusiasm of their most likely successors and probably lose them; they then eventually have to hand over their task to those who have had to wait too long for the responsibility and who have not been properly prepared for it. Timing is fundamentally important. Better to hand over too early than too late. Leadership involves the ability to know when to bow out.

The test of the effectiveness of your leadership is whether on your relinquishing the work for which you have been responsible it bears not so much your mark but God's.

A sphere of personal power

Leadership ought never to be regarded as a stepping-stone to the achievement of personal ambitions. It is to be accepted for the sake of our Lord Jesus Christ and others rather than out of motives of personal advancement and prestige.

The kudos of leadership may incline people to try to hang on to responsibility for the sake of their enjoyment of the position. To this end they may appoint as subordinates and colleagues those who will either follow them blindly or share their point of view. They will be suspicious of potential colleagues who may disturb affairs by freshness of approach and ideas.

If people gain the impression that to get on with you they must always see eye to eye with you, you have failed as a leader. If you appreciate having around you only those who always agree with you, as king of your self-built castle, your sphere of power rests upon shaky foundations. Avoid this peril at all costs. Much as you may enjoy the privileges of leadership, hold to them lightly.

Becoming an idol

Our contemporary world delights to make prominent individuals 'stars' and the 'stars' may love it. But Christian leaders are not to be 'stars' but believers who reflect the mind and character of their Lord. Towards the end of his ministry, Robert Murray M'Cheyne was fearful of becoming an idol to his people; for he was loved and respected by many who gave no evidence of love for the Lord Jesus Christ. This often pained him. It is understandable and appropriate for people to develop a very special love for their spiritual leaders, but danger is always at hand. M'Cheyne used to say, 'Ministers are but the pole; it is to the brazen serpent you are to look.'

There is much to be thankful for when people appreciate and admire the contribution you make. Nevertheless, there are three good reasons why any kind of hero-worship should be discouraged.

• It will do your pride no good, for your pride will enjoy every flattering remark.

- It will do those whom you lead no good, for they will lose their sense of dependence upon God through their dependence upon you.
- When the time comes for the appointment of your successor, you will have made that person's task difficult, for people will consider an effective replacement impossible.

Demonstrate by wise delegation that other people can do some of the jobs you do. Try to have everything functioning without being the kingpin in any individual part. Bring your colleagues in leadership to the fore as much as possible. As you do practical things like this, sensitive to the danger of becoming an idol, that appreciation which encourages and helps you to do your job will remain without going to the harmful extreme of 'idolatry'.

Remember

Dr Colin Roberts remembered Dr Sangster saying, 'These gifts of drive, leadership, power to get things done, entrusted to some of us, can so easily become sub-Christian or even non-Christian.'[4] Here is the greatest peril for leaders: they may become so caught up with their leadership that it runs away with them and becomes an end in itself. Not only must leaders be watchful of the spiritual welfare of those whom they lead but also of themselves (Acts 20:28), for they are subject to unique temptations and attacks from the devil. Provide opportunity for self-examination to ensure that your gifts of leadership are used to spiritual ends and not to ambitions and objectives dictated by your lower nature.

Remember that all Christians, and leaders in particular, are to live and work as those who must give account (Hebrews 13:17). Your joy and satisfaction must not be so much in your service but in Jesus Christ himself (Romans 15:17). What matters is not so much the reputation with which you ultimately retire from leadership but the honour which your people give to our Lord Jesus Christ. Thomas Jefferson, the United States President, was realistic about public office. 'I have learnt to expect that it will rarely fall to the lot of imperfect man to retire from this station (*the presidency*) with the reputation and favour which bring him into it.'[5] Dag Hammorskjold, former head of the UN, significantly and tellingly wrote, 'Around a man who has been pushed into the limelight, a legend begins to grow as it does around a dead man. But a dead man is in no danger of yielding to the temptation to nourish his legend, or accept its picture as reality. I pity the man who falls in love with his image as it is drawn by public opinion during the honeymoon of publicity.'[6]

Prayer

Heavenly Father, please deliver me from the pride that feels that perils that beset others will not come to me. May I love the tasks you give me not because of any prominence that they give but because they are a means of honouring the Lord Jesus to whom I owe more than everything. Help me to be sensitive to your Spirit when he would alert me to a danger or snare into which I may fall. I ask this in the name of the Lord Jesus. Amen.

Questions for Bible study groups

Read Isaiah 3:12; 9:14-16; Luke 12:35-48

1. *Isaiah 3:12; 9:14-16*: Upon what serious faults of leadership do these verses focus? Can you remember occasions when the Lord Jesus warned people against this failing? (For example, see Matthew 15:14; 18:6.)
2. *Luke 12:35-48*: What paramount attitude does our Lord Jesus Christ urge us to adopt? If the manager and servant represent Christian leaders, what qualities in them are commended in this passage?
3. What do you consider to be the main peril of leadership and why?

Questions for church leaders

1. *Are there other perils of leadership we want to add?*
2. *How do we foster a right sense of accountability for one another?*
3. *Would we resent being challenged by one of our colleagues in leadership about our attitudes and actions?*
4. *How do we encourage and maintain accountability?*
5. *What are the best antidotes to pride?*

15.
Pluses of Christian leadership

Most biographies of leaders in the secular world, while acknowledging the downside of leadership, reveal a sense of privilege. This awareness should be even more acute in Christian leaders since there are very special 'pluses' in Christian leadership.

A privileged succession

Think of those who have passed on the baton of leadership to you. They in turn could identify the people who did the same for them. How remarkable it would be if you could trace the story of this back through the centuries. You would find yourself linked to Moses and the patriarchs in the Old Testament and the apostles in the New, as well as to many heroes of the faith in church history. Your present-day privilege is to pass the baton on to the next generation.

God's presence and help

As we trace the story of the leadership God has raised up during the centuries, one of the distinct features has been his reassurance to leaders of his presence and help. Moses had the confidence to declare to those under his leadership, 'Be strong and courageous. Do not be afraid or terrified … for the LORD your God goes with you; he will never leave you nor forsake you' (Deuteronomy 31:6).

Essential to the Lord Jesus' parting words to the leaders to whom he had devoted himself was the encouragement, 'Surely I am with you always, to the very end of the age' (Matthew 28:20). When Paul knew opposition to his ministry, 'One night the Lord spoke to Paul in a vision: "Do not be afraid; keep on speaking, do not be silent. For I am with you, and no-one is going to attack and harm you, because I have many people in this city."' Little wonder that 'Paul stayed for a year and a half, teaching them the word of God' (Acts 18:9-11).

The most immediate helpline

Helplines are available to our contemporary world by correspondence, e-mail, web sites, telephones and mobiles, but none is more immediate than the privilege of prayer. When Moses despaired about the people he was called to lead, his resort and strength came from calling upon God in prayer. The Lord Jesus taught the disciples to pray, prompted as they were to want to pray because they saw the place it had in their Master's life. Paul's letters are full of teaching on prayer and actual prayers that he offered to God.

When the apostles determined the need to recognize leaders in the early church to relieve them of some administrative duties it was so that they might give 'attention to *prayer* and the ministry of the word' (Acts 6:4). So often you will carry burdens you are meant to have but not to carry. As you find them placed upon you, perhaps for individuals or aspects of your work, your immediate privilege is to seek the help of your heavenly Father in the name of your Saviour. As others share their concerns and burdens your privilege is to say there and then, 'Let us pray together about them.' Daniel exercised a position of strategic leadership and was no doubt extremely busy, but the only fault those who opposed his leadership could identify was that he prayed three times a day (Daniel 6:10-11)!

The perfect example to follow

Secular leadership seminars will suggest a variety of techniques and patterns. It would be presumptuous and foolish to suggest that these have no value. But a real plus of Christian leadership is that you know whose example you are to follow at all times and without exception — that of the Lord Jesus Christ.

The New Testament constantly brings his example before us and calls us to follow it and to fix our eyes upon him. You can face every difficulty and meet every demand as your eyes are upon him.

An exceptional fellowship

Christian leadership brings you into a remarkable fellowship with God, with your colleagues in leadership and those whom you serve. Peter significantly describes Christian leaders under the title of 'shepherds' and refers to the Lord Jesus Christ as 'the Chief Shepherd' (1 Peter 5:2, 4). In other words, Christian leaders have the special privilege of fulfilling and continuing the work of the Lord Jesus, the Great Shepherd of his flock, and they know a special fellowship with him as they fulfil that function.

As you give yourself to your God-given task you develop and enjoy an exceptional fellowship with your colleagues in leadership. It is a fellowship in the Lord Jesus, prompted and maintained by the Holy Spirit, and is intended to enrich you in all the ups and downs of your work. Some of your richest memories of such fellowship will be when you have been up against it in some way and you have knelt to pray together. The interesting thing will be that as you reflect upon it, perhaps years afterwards, you will not remember the difficulties but you will relish the memory of the fellowship. As you serve others as a leader you develop a very special relationship with them. It is one of trust and of love. It is a great encouragement to be trusted and loved.

The liberating factor

To lead others in the secular world means that you are always under the scrutiny of others who may either have too high expectations of you or who may misjudge you and your performance. It can be an alarming snare for it may cause you to be always looking over your shoulder so that you live on a razor's edge of uncertainty.

How different is Christian leadership! Although both those whom you lead and your companions in leadership may sometimes misunderstand or misjudge you, the one you ultimately serve, the Chief Shepherd, never misinterprets your motives or misunderstands you. While you are to be concerned to do what is right and to show where possible that is what you are doing, you are not to live with the esteem of others as the priority of your life but with an eye above everything to the approval of the Lord Jesus. This is a gloriously liberating factor! If you live with your eyes upon human approval, you will often be misunderstood and the fear of their disapproval will prove to be a dreadful snare. If your eyes are on the Chief Shepherd, you will know liberty and joy!

The unique reward

In the same passage where Peter writes of the privilege of being a shepherd of Christ's flock, he reminds his readers of the special reward that is before those who prove themselves to be faithful overseers: 'And when the Chief Shepherd appears, you will receive the crown of glory that will never fade away' (1 Peter 5:4). Faithfulness is equated with willing, eager and humble service with no greediness for personal profit or gain and most of all with being an example to those whom you lead (1 Peter 5:2-3). No definition of that crown of glory is given because it is simply beyond words to express. At its very least it will mean that you 'will share in the glory to be revealed' (1 Peter 5:1).

Prayer

Lord Jesus, who has given me such a tremendous privilege in being able to serve you and your people, help me to want no reward other than to know that I please you; help me to finish the race and complete the task you have given me. For your glory's sake, Amen.

Questions for Bible study groups

Read Hebrews 11; Deuteronomy 31:6; Matthew 28:20; Acts 18:9-11

1. Hebrews 11 brings before us the men and women of faith in the Old Testament. Which of them would you regard as leaders? The chapter does not have as its purpose the display of the pluses of leadership but as you go through the list can you think of any pluses that these individuals knew?
2. *Deuteronomy 31:6; Matthew 28:20; Acts 18:9-11:* These verses all point to a particular plus we all may covet. Do you think this benefit is particularly linked with obedient service?
3. Are there any pluses of Christian leadership you can add? Which do you consider to be the most wonderful?

Questions for church leaders

1. *Are we as leaders finding the help we need and which God wants us to have through prayer, and particularly in praying together?*
2. *Do we deliberately and consciously relate any challenge and difficulty to the Bible's teaching on the issue?*
3. *What can we do to cultivate greater fellowship amongst ourselves?*

References

Chapter 1: The necessity for leadership
1. *Ego*, Edition 13, March 2004, The London Institute for Contemporary Christianity, p.6.
2. Colin Powell, *A Soldier's Way*, Hutchison, p.264.
3. Harry Reid, *Outside Verdict — An Old Kirk in a New Scotland*, St Andrew Press, Edinburgh, p.90.
4. David Francis, *But Above All*, Epworth Press, p.66f.
5. David Sheppard, *Steps along Hope Street*, Hodder and Stoughton, p.30.

Chapter 2: Essential qualities for spiritual leadership
1. Rudolph Giuliani, *Leadership*, Little, Brown, p.226f.
2. Elspeth Huxley, *Peter Scott*, Faber, p.200.

Chapter 6: Basic practice
1. Jeremy Paxman, *The English*, Michael Joseph, p.134.
2. Charles Warr, *Glimmering Landscape*, Hodder and Stoughton, p.83.
3. Margaret Drewery, *William Carey — Shoemaker and Missionary*, Hodder and Stoughton, 1978, p.36.

4. CBE Harrison, *Life and Belief in the experience of John W. Laing*, Hodder and Stoughton, p.32.

Chapter 7: Good personal relationships
1. Denis Healey, *The Time of my Life*, Michael Joseph, p.28.
2. J. Pollock, *Hudson Taylor and Maria*, Hodder and Stoughton, p.116.
3. Joan Haslip, *Parnell. A biography*, Cobden-Sanderson, London, 1936, p.183.
4. Powell, *A Soldier's Way*, p.395.
5. Pollock, *Hudson Taylor and Maria*, p.35.
6. Paul Sangster, *Dr Sangster*, Epworth Press, p.253.

Chapter 8: Delegation
1. Roy Hattersley, *Blood and Fire*, Little, Brown, p.249.
2. Reid, *Outside Verdict*, p.144.
3. Betty Lee Skinner, *Daws — a Man who trusted God*, Zondervan, p.328f.
4. Timothy Dudley-Smith, *John Stott — The Making of a Leader*, IVP, p.274.
5. Basil Matthews, *John R. Mott*, Student Christian Movement, p.76.
6. Dudley-Smith, *Stott — The Making of a Leader*, p.288.
7. Giuliani, *Leadership*, p.314.
8. Imogen Lycett Green, *Grandmother's Footsteps, A Journey in search of Penelope Betjeman*, Macmillan, 1994, p.17.

Chapter 9: Efficiency
1. Charles E. Fox, *Kakamora*, Hodder and Stoughton, p.16.
2. Powell, *A Soldier's Way*, p.109.
3. Russell Hitt, *Jungle Pilot*, Hodder and Stoughton, p.173.

4. Thor Heyerdahl, *In the Footsteps of Adam*, Little, Brown, p.111.
5. Dudley-Smith, *Stott — The Making of a Leader*, p.109.
6. Sheppard, *Steps along Hope Street*, p.122.

Chapter 10: Colleagues
1. Tracy Edwards, *Living Every Second*, Hodder and Stoughton, p.166.
2. Roger Steer, *J. Hudson Taylor, A Man in Christ*, OMF Books, p.341.

Chapter 12: Chairmanship
1. Timothy Dudley-Smith, *John Stott: A Global Ministry*, IVP, p.213.

Chapter 13: Problems
1. John Beames, *Memoirs of a Bengal Civilian,* Chatto and Windus, p.151.
2. Andrew Thomson, *John Owen: The Prince of the Puritans,* Christian Focus, p.142.
3. Hitt, *Jungle Pilot*, p.221.
4. Skinner, *Daws*, p.118.

Chapter 14: Perils
1. Steer, *J. Hudson Taylor,* p.320.
2. Powell, *A Soldier's Way*, p.243f.
3. Betty Boothroyd, *The Autobiography*, Century, p.65.
4. Sangster, *Dr Sangster*, p.284.
5. Powell, *A Soldier's Way*, p.481.
6. Dag Hammorskjold, *Markings*, New York, Alfred A. Knopf, 1946, p.66.

Scripture index

A wide range of excellent books on spiritual subjects is available from Evangelical Press. Please write to us for your free catalogue or contact us by e-mail.

Evangelical Press
Faverdale North, Darlington, DL3 0PH, England

e-mail: sales@evangelicalpress.org

Evangelical Press USA
P. O. Box 825, Webster, New York 14580, USA

e-mail: usa.sales@evangelicalpress.org

web: http://www.evangelicalpress.org